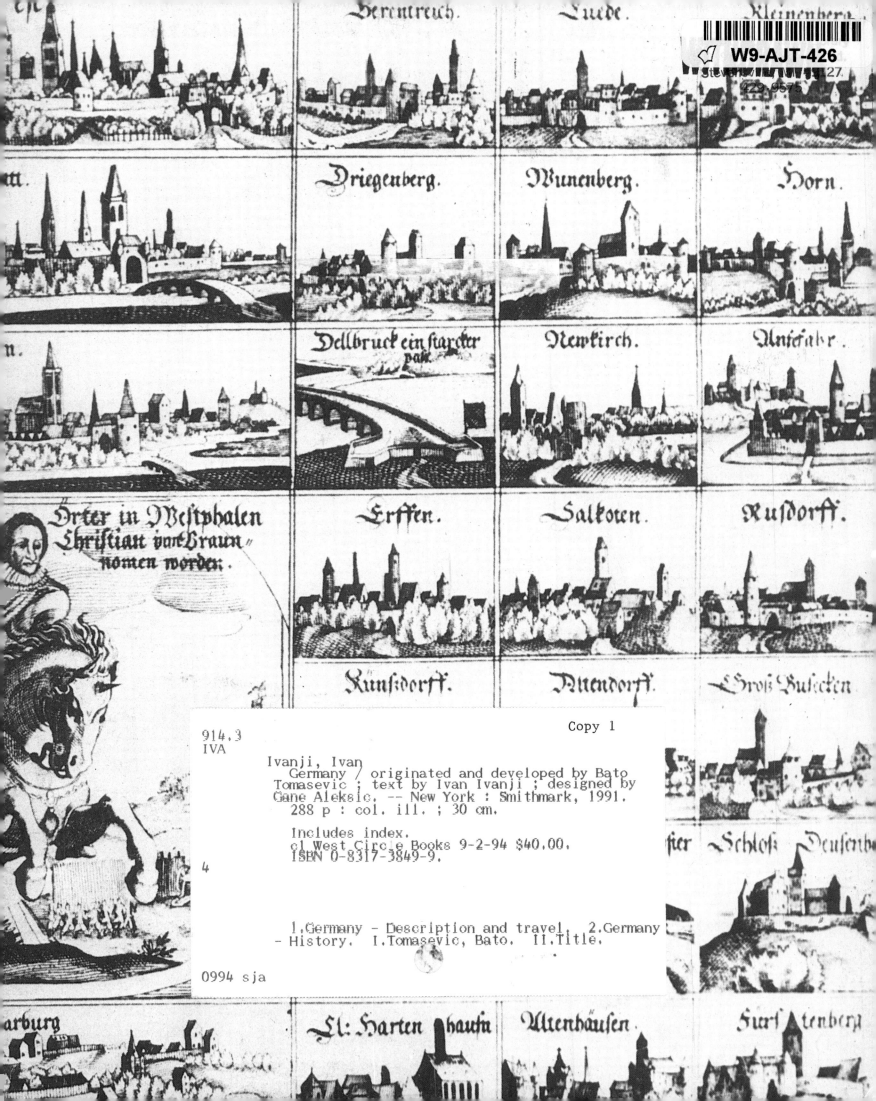

GERM

Originated and developed by

BATO TOMAŠEVIĆ

Text by

IVAN IVANJI

Designed by

GANE ALEKSIĆ

SMITHMARK

For SMITHMARK Edition
© World copyright 1991
FLINT RIVER PRESS, Ltd., London

First published in the United States
in 1991
by SMITHMARK PUBLISHERS INC.
112 Madison Avenue, New York,
NY 10016
All rights reserved.

ISBN 0-8317-3849-9

Text and captions:
IVAN IVANJI

Photographs:
ANDREA LUPPI
MARCO CODUTTI
DJORDJE ĆUBRILO
ROBERT HARDING PICTURE
LIBRARY, London

Translator:
KARIN RADOVANOVIĆ

Editor:
MADGE PHILLIPS

SMITHMARK books are available for
bulk purchase for sales promotion
and premium use. For details write
or telephone the Manager of Special
Sales, SMITHMARK Publishers Inc.,
112 Madison Avenue, New York,
NY 10016. (212) 532-6600.

Printed and bound in Yugoslavia by
DELO, Ljubljana

CONTENTS

HEARTLAND OF EUROPE

I T IS INCONTESTABLE that no other major European country has had such an unsettled position, such shifting boundaries, as Germany, making it difficult to define precisely how far it actually extends. Perhaps for this very reason, no other country has caused its neighbors so much distress, involving them in all kinds of upheavals, bloodshed and war. All this is interconnected: if borders cannot be traced along a river, sea or mountain range, they will be not only flexible, but disputed, and this has always had historical consequences. The fortunes of a nation are inextricably bound up with its geography and history.

But while there are different views on the question of Germany's precise geographical extent, all are agreed on one point – it is the heartland of Europe. This, however, is not sufficient, though the more one dwells on the problem, the more elusive the answer – as became particularly evident when planning this book, in the final decade of the present millennium. If the book had been started even half a year earlier, it would have opened with the fact that the territory in Europe which people for centuries have been accustomed to call Germany comprised two sovereign states inhabited by Germans. Now, all of a sudden, to the surprise of even the best informed, most far-sighted statesmen, we are again speaking of a single, united Germany.

As German reference books explained until recently, "Since a peace treaty was not signed after the Second World War, and there is no common German government, the name Germany is used to refer to the German *Reich* within its borders of 1938..." These borders, however, incorporated parts of present-day Poland, and even the Soviet Union, and few, except for a handful of hard-core German nationalists, would venture to include these areas in Germany today. It appears fairly certain that this large, new, united Germany will have a permanent 'natural' boundary in the east along the Oder and Neisse rivers. Here at least is one natural border for the part of the world being described.

Another, which can scarcely be disputed, is created by the two seas in the north: the Baltic, which Germans call the East (Ostsee), and the North Sea, part of the great Atlantic Ocean. Between these extends the peninsula of Jutland, forming the central part of another country, Denmark. A different kind of barrier marks off northern Jutland and the Danish islands from Germany: here the border is not formed by water, nor is Jutland separated by a range of mountains; the two countries are set apart by the use of different languages. In the south, however, even this criterion cannot serve as a distinction, since the same language is spoken in two neighboring countries, by the Austrians and northern Swiss, who share a common literary language, though the local dialects

1. The fairy-tale castle of Neuschwanstein, one of the world's most fantastic edifices, took 17 years to complete (1869–1886). Its name 'new swan's rock' refers to the lake below, the Schwansee, with its many swans. This fabulous turreted castle in neo-Romanesque style perched on a high rock was conceived by the eccentric Bavarian king, Ludwig II, and designed by the theater painter C. Jank. The King's private apartments were decorated with scenes from epic tales used by Wagner in his operas.

2. Landscape near Mittenwald (Bavaria), close to the Austrian frontier, a region of lofty alpine peaks, glacial lakes and picturesque villages, ideal for mountain climbing, hiking and winter sports. ▷

3. A typical Bavarian church with an 'onion dome' in the Schwangau area. Schwan means 'swan', and many of these graceful creatures glide on the nearby lakes. The Bavarians, predominantly Catholic, were coverted to Christianity by wandering Scottish and Irish friars (from a monastery in Burgundy) early in the 7th century. The priests in these small churches still play an important role in everyday, and even political, life. ▷▷

differ. Yet in terms of dialectical features the Bavarians, who are unquestionably German, are much closer to the Austrians than to the Germans of the north. All one can say is that the southern German borders evolved more or less accidentally, and have been maintained for centuries, winding through valleys and over the spurs of the skyscraping Alps.

It is in the west, however, that it is hardest, from a geographical or even historical standpoint, to determine where Germany ends. A linguistic barrier, as with Denmark, establishes the frontiers with the Netherlands and Belgium. But in the most sensitive sector, over which numerous wars have been fought, it is not at all clear where Germany ends and France begins. The provinces of Alsace and Lorraine (Lothringen), which were finally ceded to France after two world wars, for centuries had a population speaking predominantly German, as many of their inhabitants still do. Here the borders were political decisions.

Politics will eventually put an end to all uncertainty. On January 1, 1993, when customs officers no longer wave down travelers, and Europeans can cross borders freely without even noticing what country they are in, citizens of a united Europe will no longer give a thought to what divided them in the past.

GEOGRAPHICALLY, Germany, the heartland of Europe, comprises four major physical divisions: the north German plain, the central or mid-German highlands, southern Germany with the valleys of the Main and Neckar, and the Bavarian Alps and plateau.

This is the picture today, though this part of the world once presented a very different aspect. During the Ice Ages and between them, periods of extreme climate succeeded one another, much colder and hotter than any recorded in historical times. These, now inconceivable, climatic oscillations cannot be attributed to nuclear experiments or damage to the ozone layer, for there was no one to engage in nuclear experimentation or to pollute the environment, no one even to worry about it. Much more powerful forces were at work — the forces of nature. There were periods when rhinoceros wallowed in the cooling mud of the Rhine, when lions prowled in the dense forests of the present-day Ruhr, but also periods when glaciers not only capped mountain peaks but descended to the banks of the Danube. It was only when these glacial sheets finally retreated that the relief we know today emerged, that the great rivers forged their present courses, leaving in Germany, as reminders of that age, only a few lakes in Bavaria.

GERMANS LIKE TO CALL THE RHINE their 'river of destiny', though barely half of it (440 out of a total 820 miles) is in Germany. The Rhine rises in Switzerland and, after leaving Germany, flows north through the Netherlands before emptying into the North Sea. Numerous tributaries swell the river, making it one of Europe's most important inland waterways. Many German poems and legends are associated with it, while the picturesque hilltop castles along its banks make it particularly attractive for visitors.

According to legend, the siren Lorelei used to sit on a rock above the Rhine, combing her long golden hair. Entranced by her beauty, fishermen would forget to watch out for underwater reefs, run aground, and drown in the river. This was most memorably described by the son of a Jewish family of Düsseldorf, Heinrich Heine. Literally every German child can recite at least the beginning of his poem, "Ich weiss nicht was soll es bedeuten, dass ich so traurig bin..." (I know not why I should be so sad...). Under Hitler it was forbidden to publish, even read, anything

4

4, 5. *Neuschwanstein castle looks different from every angle. It was in order to pay for this and other ruinously expensive projects that King Ludwig II agreed to accept the Prussian king as German emperor in exchange for a large sum of money offered by Bismarck.*

6. Jakobsbrunnen (Jacob's fountain) has stood on the main square of the Bavarian town of Straubing since 1664. Behind it rises the town clock tower, a singular Gothic construction with five 220-foot pinnacles. The town is noted for its churches, medieval dwellings and fine mansions from the 16th and 17th centuries, testifying to the prosperity of its burghers.

7. Munich, the capital of Bavaria, is also known as the 'capital with a heart' or the 'northernmost Mediterranean city'— all ways of saying that it has more charm and

8

warmth than most cities of the north. Munich's landmark is the Frauenkirche, with 120-foot twin towers characterized by their unusual Baroque cupolas. Illuminated at night, its silhouette rises high above the surrounding buildings.

8. The National Theater in Munich on Max Joseph Square is the home of the famous Bavarian State Opera. The original building, where many of Richard Wagner's operas were first performed, was demolished during the war. Its restoration was considered a priority by the people of Munich.

9

10

BROTPREISE

Doppelbrot	1.20
5er Brezen	3.50
10er Brezen	5.50
Zwiebelbrot	3.—
Vintschgauer	3.—
Wachauerweckerl	
Käsestangen	2,50

9–11. *Every autumn from mid-September to early October, Munich organizes its October Festival (Oktoberfest) on the Theresienwiesen not far from the middle of the city. Once these festivities began with a carriage race. Today it is a huge fair where merrymakers from all over the world consume up to 10 million pints of beer (for which Bavaria is justly renowned), tons of sausages, mounds of pretzels and other specialties.*

13

12, 13. Königsee (King's Lake), one of the loveliest lakes in Germany. Nestling amid the towering Watzman and Jenner peaks, it has an area of 3.2 square miles. Popular for all kinds of water sports in summertime, in winter when frozen the lake is perfect for skating.

14

14, 15.   On his way to the Königsee the motorist will turn off the crowded highway and suddenly find himself in an enchanted world. On a tiny peninsula stands the chapel of St Bartholomew, built in the shape of a four-leafed clover, its silhouette a symbol of the lake, which is connected in the south with the Obersee and the Röthbachfall cascades.

16, 18.   Immenstadt (Bavaria) is one of many small places where ancient traditions have been preserved and where folk costume – for men, short leather pants, white shirt and green feather-trimmed hat – has remained workaday dress. Livestock fairs are still important here. One of the curiosities of a festivity marking the return of the livestock from summer pastures in the mountains is 'measuring the beard'. While away, the herders do not shave, and when they descend to Immenstadt in the fall, their beards are measured, the longest and finest winning a prize.

17.   The customary drink in the Immenstadt area, as elsewhere in Bavaria, is beer, but posted on the beergarden wall are the pious words: 'Mother Anne, help us!'

17

19. Passau lies on three rivers, at the spot where the Inn and the Iltz flow into the Danube, which is navigable from this point. This ancient town, the seat of a bishop since 739, has many hotels and inns to accommodate passengers setting out on cruises down the Danube to the Black Sea.

20. Passau's Baroque cathedral of St
Stephen was built after a fire which
destroyed most of the old Gothic church in
1662. Its organ with 17,300 pipes is the
biggest in the world. The bronze bell
weighs 17,290 pounds, (7859 kg) the
heaviest in Bavaria.

21

21, 22. Neuburg an der Donau is dominated by its great Schloss, in early German Renaissance style, mostly from the 16th century. Its chapel, painted with frescoes (1543), is one of the earliest Protestant palace chapels in Germany. The proximity of Austria and Czechoslovakia has influenced the local cuisine, which means more noodles, dumplings, heavier wines, grilled meat. In its upper reaches the Danube is still clean enough to provide fresh-water fish.

JOANNI NEPOMUCENO
IN TERRIS
FAMÆ
IN AQUIS
VITÆ
PATRONOMIRABILI
DEVOTI
CLIENTES
M D C C V I I

23, 24. Painted ceiling of the church of Maria Viktoria, generally known as the Asamkirche, in Ingolstadt on the Danube. A fine example of German Rococo, completed in 1736, it was probably designed by the famous Cosmas Damian Asam, who definitely painted the trompe l'oeil frescoes that cover the entire ceiling, creating an illusion of limitless space.

25, 26. Smaller towns in Germany look very much alike. (This is Ulm). Almost every one has an old church and an impressive castle nearby — for Germany consisted of numerous principalities, duchies or counties, and if there was no secular ruler, medieval bishops vied in raising fine buildings. Invariably there is a square with an attractive fountain or monument. Since many towns were bombed during the Second World War, the damaged buildings were either painstakingly restored or new ones carefully matched with the earlier style.

27

27. A house in typical alpine style in Oberammergau (Bavaria), famous for the Passion play depicting Christ's life, death and resurrection. It has been performed here once every 10 years since 1634, when the villagers, spared by a visitation of the plague, vowed to re-enact Christ's Passion as an expression of gratitude and in the hope of being spared future epidemics. Only people born in Oberammergau or residents of 20 years' standing can take part in the performances, held since 1930 in a specially built theater.

28

28. The German phrase durch die Blume sagen, unlike the English 'say it with flowers', means to say something unpleasant in a polite, roundabout way on occasions when stronger expressions would be more appropriate. Once every flower had a special meaning in Germany, and messages or news could be conveyed by sending certain blooms. In colloquial speech people say, '...thanks for the flowers'', when rejecting criticism. Though idioms change, flowers remain important in everyday life in Germany.

34

29.   This gentleman from Baden-Baden is
a typical representative of the south
German. His hair, moustache and bearded
cheeks (Backenbart in German) are
a symbol of masculinity, while the
carefully shaven chin reflects his neatness.
Most people in this region feel that
traditional customs should be preserved
while aiming for a modern way of life. In
this respect the inhabitants of Bavaria,
Württemburg and Swabia differ little from
the Austrians and German-speaking Swiss.

31

30. A watermill in Ulm, a town on the Danube which was formerly an imperial city, an important center of trade from the 12th century on. The Gothic Münster (cathedral), one of the most important and largest religious buildings in Europe, was begun in 1370. The old town center with its fine town hall and half-timbered houses reflects its medieval prosperity.

31. An especially fine example of a half-timbered house in the town of Bacharach on the Rhine. Here the entire wooden construction is visible on the façade. Carved and painted ornamentation further enhance the decorative effect.

32, 33.   During the summer the lakes of Bavaria – here Chiemsee – are ideal for water sports, especially sailing. With streams flowing into them from glaciers and mountains, the lakes have a natural system of purification protecting them from the onslaught of tourists from Bavarian towns.
Along a wide expressway, the lake is easily reached from Munich.

33

34.   Mt. Tegelberg in the Schwangau region has an observation deck and tavern reached by cable car at an altitude of 5730 feet. This makes it an ideal spot for hang-gliding, a highly popular sport in Germany's mountainous parts. This scenic region is worth visiting not only for the pleasures of 'flying' and mountaineering, but also for its many picturesque castles.

written by a writer of Jewish descent. The lines about the Lorelei could not be banned; it was simpler to ignore its author and claim the poem was of popular origin.

Many verses associated with the Rhine mention wine, not merely because in German, as in English, the words happen to rhyme, but primarily because Rhineland or Rhenish wine enjoys international fame. The ancient Romans planted the first vines here two thousand years ago.

THE ELBE, second largest German river, also rises outside Germany, in the Czech and Slovak Republic, though its nine-mile-wide estuary is located north of Hamburg. Of its total length of 690 miles, 460 are in Germany. The lower reaches of the Elbe are navigable for ocean-going ships. The legendary spirits of the Elbe are not seated on rocks, combing their golden tresses in the evening, luring men to their death. They are perhaps even more cunning and harder to distinguish from mere mortals. When these water sprites *(Nixe)* come ashore, they dress and resemble simple, though lovely, maidens. They can be recognized by only one detail: an item of their clothing, perhaps only the edge of an apron, or in the case of modern sprites, the bottom of their jeans, remains damp and never dries. Water sprites seek the love of a mortal man, and when they find one, the besotted youth willingly follows his beloved into the murky depths of the river. After they leap into the waves, the fiancée's wreath may rise to the surface. This means that the young man has been welcomed to the underwater fairy world and will live there happily ever after. More often the surface of the water reddens with blood, a sign that the sprite's family has devoured the unfortunate young man.

THE DANUBE (Donau), Europe's largest river after the Volga, flows through Germany for only 385 of its 1790 miles, though it rises there, in the dismal-sounding Schwarzwald, the Black Forest, suggestive of the gloomy ancient German legends. Who would imagine that this spring, high in the mountains, could be the source of a great river, which in another country, Austria, inspired the lilting gaiety of the Blue Danube waltz? Things obviously undergo a considerable change when crossing from Germany into Austria, and vice versa. One of the greatest composers of all time, Ludwig van Beethoven, who lived and worked in Vienna and is associated with this city, was in fact born in Bonn, on the banks of the Rhine, not the Danube. Adolf Hitler, *Führer* and embodiment of evil in twentieth-century Germany, was not German at all, but born in Austria, at Braunau on the Inn, a tributary of the Danube. When a German remarked to the Austrian premier that it was fortunate for his countrymen that the world thought Beethoven to be Austrian and did not know that Hitler really was, Prime Minister Wranitzky replied, "Only, please, don't forget that Hitler in our country was a housepainter and vagabond, and in your country you made him chancellor."

Germany's three largest rivers are primarily European waterways. The Rhine and the Elbe, receiving numberless tributaries, drain water from the northwest into the windswept foggy ocean, while the Danube heads in the opposite direction and links the country of its source with the continental southeast, emptying into the Black Sea. The recently completed system of canals linking the Rhine, Main and Danube provides a shortcut through the center of the continent. Ships can now sail from the North to the Black Sea without taking the circuitous maritime route.

In Germany the Rhine drains 72,230 square miles of territory, the Elbe 57,780, and the Danube 31,000 square miles. This means that most of the other German rivers flow into one of these 'big three'. The principal tributaries of the Rhine are the Main and the Moselle (Mosel), their sloping

35. *Berchtesgaden, a resort in upper Bavaria at an altitude of 1890 feet, below Mt. Watzmann (9040 feet). The village is known for its woodcarvers and has a school of applied arts. To the east rises Obersalzberg (Upper Salt Mountain), where Hitler built his inaccessible Eagle's Nest. Here he spent his free time, received visitors of state, and planned further conquests together with his generals.*

banks famed for their vineyards. Also draining into the Rhine are the Neckar in the south and the Ruhr in northern Germany. The latter gave its name to the Ruhr region, the site of what was until recently a mighty steel industry based on rich coal deposits. The second group of rivers, in the eastern half of Germany, includes the Spree, which flows through Berlin, and the Havel, which joins the Elbe and continues on to the North Sea. All these waterways are linked by canals, forming a network of communications important for Germany's economy.

Once the Oder and the Neisse were considered German rivers; today, as we have seen, the world views them as state frontiers. The Neisse is a tributary of the Oder and flows into the Baltic at Szczecin.

THE NORTHERN SEAS differ from those further south – the Mediterranean or the Carribean. Swirling clouds of fog often hide the endless expanses of grey water. The marshy coastal belt west of Jutland is protected by the string of Frisian Islands, divided among Germany, the Netherlands and Denmark. To Germany belong the East Frisians and part of the North Frisian group. Until drawn to southern climes, Germans used to vacation here in the summertime, most of them strolling along the beaches or building sand-castles rather than actually bathing in the cold, choppy waves. The largest island is Sylt (58 square miles). Without constant work on the embankments protecting its western coast from storms and strong tides, it would soon shrink and disappear altogether. The Baltic shore is similar, but better protected from the ocean, so that the winds are not so strong and the tides less destructive. The coastal belt here abounds in lakes.

Between 1887 and 1895 a canal was dug across the peninsula of Jutland, first named after Kaiser Wilhelm, but now generally known as the Kiel Canal, as its eastern end on the Baltic Sea begins just north of the city of Kiel. Nearly 60 miles long, it shortens the voyage from the Baltic to the North Sea.

Here in the north of Germany one ponders once again the effect of nature and geographical conditions on man's life. Scandinavian and Anglo-Saxon mores unquestionably bear a resemblance to the customs of northern Germany, which are very different from those of the southern regions.

Germans have a special feeling for the small island of Heligoland (Helgoland), lying furthest northwest in the North Sea. As legend has it, this rocky, red sandstone isle was broken off from Norway by the devil himself and cast here among the waves. The first written record of it dates from the eighth century, when Charlemagne's advisor and teacher, the learned Alcuin, described it in his biography of St Willibrord. Afterwards pirates inhabited the island and when their time passed, the tourist trade took its place – a less hazardous and at any rate more civilized way of making a living than piracy. A long list of poets and writers from all over the world came to stay here, among them Heinrich von Kleist and Heinrich Heine. It was on Heligoland that Hoffmann von Fallersleben wrote *Deutschlandlied* (Song of the Germans) and sold it to the publisher Campe for only four gold coins, never imagining it would become the German national anthem. Swedish playwright August Strindberg married his Frieda on this island. Held for a time by Denmark and then Britain, in 1890 Heligoland returned to German hands, though to get it back Kaiser Wilhelm was obliged to cede the colony of Zanzibar to his cousin Queen Victoria. In 1935 Hitler began to convert the island into a military base against Great Britain, which bombed it heavily when war broke out. After the war the British Royal Air Force used it as a base, and it was not until 1952 that Heligoland, still lying in ruins, was restored to Germany and repopulated. It subsequently developed as a resort, though mostly for short excursions, since few people want to spend their holidays exposed to the strong winds blowing almost continually off the Atlantic.

LAKES. Germany has only twenty or so with an area exceeding one square mile, and only two of any great size. The largest by far, shared with Switzerland and Austria, is the Bodensee, otherwise known as Lake Constance or the Swabian Sea (Schwäbische Meer). Lying in the Alps, 1299 feet above sea level, it has an area of 207 square miles and a maximum depth of 827 feet. The Rhine flows through it, entering near Bregenz and leaving the lake at Stein am Rhein.

The second largest lake, Grosse Müritz (45 square miles in area), is less well known, especially in recent times, since it is located in Mecklenburg, in the eastern part of Germany. It, too, has a river flowing through it: the Elde, a tributary of the Elbe.

The lovely Bavarian lakes — the Chiemsee, Starnberger See, Ammersee, Tegernsee and others — their shores dotted with castles, are all near the capital of Bavaria, Munich (München). The romantic, unbalanced, Bavarian King Ludwig (Louis) II (1845–1886) was the greatest castle builder of his age. His most memorable undertaking, the fairy-tale Neuschwanstein (New Swan Rock), was possibly an inspiration for Tchaikovsky's Swan Lake. Neglecting affairs of state and devoting more and more time and money to his obsession with the arts, Ludwig ordered the construction of Herrenchiemsee castle, on an isle in the lake of Chiemsee, as a copy of Versailles. Eventually he was declared insane, and shortly after drowned in the Starnberger See. Officially, it was suicide, but many suspected foul play.

THE CLIMATE OF GERMANY is unusual for Europe in being warmer in the north than in the south, where the Alps and the cold mountain winters influence the climate in the valleys as well. An uncommon phenomenon in this region is the *Föhn*, its name coming from the Latin *favonius* (west wind), though most people do not think of the *Föhn* as

Mechanization of agriculture in the mid-19th century: a steam-driven threshing machine.

a wind. It is, in fact, a vertical stream of warm air from the mountains, occurring when the barometric pressure north of the Alps is lower than the air pressure south of the mountains. It is most noticeable around the Bavarian lakes, but also affects the cities. People sensitive to the *Föhn* easily grow depressed and complain of headaches, or go to the opposite extreme, becoming abnormally aggressive. During the *Föhn* statisticians have recorded a significant increase in the number of road accidents, suicides and acts of violence. The milder climate of the north is attributed to the effect of the Gulf Stream, its warm air penetrating from the Atlantic along the Rhine and its tributaries. For this reason, the average winter in northwest Germany generally passes without snow, while the east has a rigorous continental climate, and the south is influenced by the proximity of the Alps.

GERMANY'S HIGHEST PEAK is the Zugspitze (9719 feet above sea level) in the Alps. For scenic beauty many would select the Berchtesgaden Alps. The somewhat lower range of mountains in central Germany is called the Mittelgebirge or Mid-German Highlands. The valley of the Rhine cuts through the Rhenish Slate Mountains (Rheinische Schiefergebirge), which west of the river are called the Eifel and Hunsrück, and to the east, the Taunus. Further east, bordering on the Czech and Slovak Republic, rise the Erzgebirge, on a southwest-northeast axis. In Thuringia the mountains are so beautiful that locals call them the Thuringian Alps.

''The appearance of the country differs considerably in different parts; but in general it is covered either by bristling forests or by foul swamps,'' wrote Roman historian Tacitus, describing Germany more than 1900 years ago. Most of the swamps have been drained, but woodland remains fairly characteristic of Germany, even where least expected – in the Ruhr industrial zone. Entire mountain ranges are named after forests: the Teutoburger Wald, Westerwald, Frankenwald, Thüringer Wald, Bayrischer Wald or Schwarzwald. *Wald* means 'forest', and when added to the name of a mountain, indicates that the mountain is thickly wooded. This scenic attraction, however, is in double jeopardy. The building of new communities and wide motorways has meant the felling of many trees. For a single major intersection 150,000 trees must be sacrificed. The second danger to trees comes from 'acid rain'; its chemical content from air pollution is particularly damaging to the beautiful evergreens. Only recently have people in Germany become generally conscious of the threat posed by a polluted environment to human survival.

Man's treatment of forests is only one aspect of his effect on nature. Since time immemorial man has felled woodland to sow crops. More recently, he has built embankments for protection against raging seas and

Preparing a printing press, 16th-century woodcut.

flooding rivers, drained marshes or created artificial lakes, drilled tunnels through mountains for roads and other communications, thus altering the appearance of the countryside. It is interesting that our eye is no longer offended by church steeples or towers occupying some hilltop, but we complain vigorously of spiky, skyward-pointing television towers or highways cutting a broad swathe through meadows and cornfields. In any case, what mankind has created slowly merges with the landscape, gradually becoming inseparable from it. Ports along the coast, towns springing up at crossroads, windmills and watermills, are all imprints of man's life on earth. A view of Germany – beside a river, lake or sea – must therefore include everything that has emerged as the work of human hands.

THE POPULAR IMAGE OF GERMANS is of an industrious, well-organized, highly disciplined people. Those who deny that races differ in genetic characteristics will reply that it is nature that determines behavior. The inhabitants of warmer climes for the most part have not had to work so hard to secure the basic creature comforts.

"A good soil for cereal crops, it will not grow fruit-trees..." wrote Tacitus, the first to leave a written description of Germany and its inhabitants. "It is well provided with livestock; but the animals are mostly undersized, and even the cattle lack the handsome heads that are their natural glory. It is the mere number of them that the Germans take pride in; for these are the only form of wealth they have, and are much prized. Silver and gold have been denied them – whether as a sign of divine favor or of divine wrath, I cannot say. Yet I would not positively assert that there are no deposits of gold and silver in Germany, since no one has prospected for them."

In the nineteen centuries since Tacitus, the picture has radically changed, except perhaps for the good crops of cereals. Livestock in Germany are indeed splendid and well-tended. True, gold was never discovered here, but most of the silver circulating in Europe from the tenth to the twelfth centuries was mined in the Erzgebirge mountains of Saxony. This is reflected in their very name (*Erz* = ore). But while searching for gold, the Germans found coal, and thus changed the landscape and their lives.

At first industrial development was merciless and did not spare the landscape, but in recent times the exploitation of natural resources and its effect upon the environment have been approached with greater concern. A few years ago the Germans were exceedingly proud when fish reappeared in the Rhine, and the minister for ecological affairs was shown on television taking a swim in the river. For decades, owing to the negligence primarily of the chemical industry Germany's rivers had become so polluted that their flora and fauna had been completely destroyed, and to swim in these waters was to risk your life. Following the unification of the two Germanys, doubtless the initiative and money will be found to return the Elbe, too, to its former beauty.

Three great rivers, the Danube, Rhine and Elbe, have always served not only as frontiers but also as arteries linking the bloodstreams of Latins, Slavs and Germans. In the coming decades their function as borders will probably diminish in favor of their connecting role. This will enhance Germany's significance as the heartland of Europe, though by itself Germany would not be enough: the bloodstream of the old continent needs a bigger heart than the land of the ancient Germans could provide alone.

THE IMPERIAL PAST

The Romans

IT IS DIFFICULT to speak about the history of a people in Europe without taking into consideration its neighbors, all the other nations sharing the same continent. It might be said that the Germans, or rather, their ancestors, entered history in September A.D. 9, the date of the battle in the Teutoburger Wald, when Arminius, chieftain of the Cherusci, succeeded in wiping out three Roman legions, the XVII, XVIII and XIX. Having served as an officer in the Roman army, Arminius, or Hermann as he was known to his German tribesmen, was familiar with their tactics and military skills; they knew nothing about the German method of fighting.

Arminius spread rumors about the weakness of his bands, and the Romans, commanded by Publius Quintilius Varus, set out from their fortified camp by the Weser River. Threading its way through the dense forests in torrential rain, the column had to spread out, the heavily laden baggage train barely keeping up with the troops. Concealed by the forest, the Germans picked off one Roman unit after another. When he realized he would lose his entire force, Varus killed himself by falling on his sword. Upon hearing the news in Rome, Augustus was so horrified he ordered that no Roman legions should ever again bear the numbers 17, 18 and 19.

History, it is said, is written by the victors. Here is a case when the opposite is true: shocked, yet dedicated to the truth, the Romans recorded the facts of their great defeat, and thus the Germans entered history.

Earlier, some six decades before the birth of Christ, the Rhine had become the border between the Roman empire and the Germanic tribes. On the left bank of the river the Romans fortified their settlements, the origin of the present-day cities of Cologne (Köln) and Trier. Then their mighty river fleet arrived. In A.D. 5 they sailed for the first time down the Weser and Elbe, intending to establish a new province under the name *Germania magna.* After Varus's defeat these plans were abandoned.

All the Romans wanted now was to protect the territory they had already conquered – present-day southern Germany. In A.D. 83, building a Roman version of the Maginot Line, they completed their *limes,* a 340-mile fortified border. On one side lay the Roman empire; on the other – beyond the Rhine in the west, the *limes* in the southwest and the Danube in the south – spread countless Germanic tribes: the East and West Goths, Vandals, Angles, Langobardi (Lombards), Suebi (Swabians), and many others, as far north as Scandinavia and east to the Weichsel and Bug rivers. Nevertheless, not a single Roman emperor ever enjoyed peace and security along these borders.

Many familiar with the situation in Germany today claim that a kind of spiritual demarcation line still exists between the south and the north, separating Roman Catholicism from Protestantism. More permanent than the division created between western and eastern Germany by the victors of World War II, it is marked not by a state frontier but by a fundamental distinction in temperament between northern and southern Germans.

But what connection do the ancient Germans described by Tacitus have with the Germans of today? About as much as the Greeks of Pericles' time with the people who have joined the European Community, or the Egyptians of the days of the Pharaohs with the subjects of President Mubarak.

In 375 the warlike, nomadic Huns, a non-Germanic people of obscure origin, moved westward and launched their assault against the Ostrogothic state of King Ermanaric between the Don and the Dniester, thus precipitating the great migrations of people known as the *Völkerwanderung*. For almost two hundred years the European continent was in a state of ferment. In the end the Hunnish leader Attila was defeated near present-day Troyes in France. Attila's death two years later, on the night of his wedding to a German princess, was partly the inspiration for the greatest of the German heroic epics, the *Nibelungenlied*, in which Attila appears as Etzel.

The Franks

At the time the Franks were just one of the many west Germanic tribes. Slowly but surely they became the dominant nation in Europe. In 768 their already large kingdom was inherited by a young ruler who, among his other exploits, would complete the conversion of the Germans to Christianity. Germans know him as Karl der Grosse, while the French refer to him as Charlemagne, each nation having appropriated him as its own.

After driving the Moors from present-day France and part of Spain and subjecting these territories to his rule, Charlemagne defeated the Bavarian hero Tassilo and Saxon leader Widukind, and annexed the Bavarian and Bohemian states. On Christmas Day 800, Pope Leo III crowned him emperor in the old church of St. Peter's in Rome. There is no point here in debating whether Charlemagne was a Frenchman or a German. In today's meaning of the words, he was neither, simply a god-given leader of men.

The official language at the time was Latin. Charlemagne knew it imperfectly. The common people spoke a tongue that learned Romans called *teutonica lingua*, which the Germans reduced to *thiudisk*, eventually producing the word *deutsch* for 'German'. Thus, it is only in the tenth century that the history of the country which calls itself *Deutschland* in fact begins. According to Tacitus, the Germani (from which the English word derives) were just one of many Germanic tribes. Similarly, the French call the Germans *Allemands* after another Germanic people, the Alemanni. The ancient form *thiudisk* may also survive in the adjective 'teutonic', with its connotations of something heavy and humorless. According to another version, the word *deutsch* comes from the name of a tribe, the Teutones, who one hundred years before Christ fought the advancing Romans. This is certainly the origin of the Italian name for the Germans, *tedesco*, and the English word, 'Teuton'.

During the Middle Ages Germany did not grow into a single national state like France, for example. From Charlemagne on, German kings who assumed the imperial title ruled a kind of supranational empire that

36. Eltz castle, overlooking the Eltz River, a tributary of the Mosel (Moselle). It owes its excellent state of repair to the fact that after suffering a disastrous fire it was rebuilt according to the old plans in 1920. German castles frequently belonged to brigand knights (Raubritter), who filled their coffers by attacking travelers, particularly merchants, in the late medieval period.

37. The castle of Gutenfels Pfalz. In the old German empire Pfalz was the name for a fortification serving as a residence for kings and emperors traveling about the land. For purposes of defence, forts and castles were generally situated on an elevation, overlooking a river. Lending a romantic aura to the German landscape, many of these castles are now converted into hotels and restaurants. ▷

transcended the linguistic barriers of embryonic nations and completely neglected Germany. Germany, on the other hand, while formally recognizing the emperor-king but not his real authority, soon disintegrated into a number of small separate states.

The head of the Roman Catholic Church was not merely the spiritual leader of the Christian world; the bishop of Rome also had secular prerogatives and found himself in the situation of competing for primacy with the German king, who also bore the title of Holy Roman Emperor. At times the emperor could appoint popes at will. Henry (Heinrich) III deposed three popes before bringing to the papal throne a German acceptable to himself. But after his death in 1059 it was decreed that only cardinals could elect a pope. The bitterest conflict broke out when Henry IV declared Pope Gregory VII deposed, and the pope excommunicated the emperor. As it turned out, the emperor had overestimated his power. The electors (Kurfürsten), princes who had the right to elect the German king, refused to recognize him unless he made his peace with the pope. Dressed as a penitent in a hair-shirt, approaching on his knees, Henry had to beg for forgiveness. This took place in the castle of Canossa, which explains why in Germany the phrase 'to go to Canossa' means performing an act of penance.

Relations were once again strained when Frederick (Friedrich) I, whom the Italians called Barbarossa because of his red beard, ascended the throne. In a series of campaigns, he managed to defeat all his secular enemies, notably Henry the Lion, (Heinrich der Löwe), and after several military expeditions into Italy refused to recognize that his imperial crown was a papal beneficium which the pope could grant at his pleasure. Barbarossa reduced the role of the pope to that of an exalted master of ceremonies.

Frederick Barbarossa was already sixty-three years old when he led a huge army on a crusade to the Holy Land, intending to liberate Jerusalem and thus enhance his prestige in the Christian world. He passed easily through Hungary and Serbia, concluding military and political alliances with local dignitaries and sparing his soldiers. He arrived triumphantly in Asia Minor and then accidentally drowned in the Saleph River. The Germans simply could not believe that such a mighty ruler could suddenly vanish. Legends sprang up, saying that he had only temporarily retired, that he was sitting in a cave in the Kyffhäuser mountains, his beard growing through a stone table, but would return to unite Germany.

Barbarossa's grandson Frederick II was well educated, interested in the natural sciences, and wrote lyric poems in Italian. At his orders books were translated from Greek, Hebrew, even Arabic, thus anticipating the Renaissance in the first half of the thirteenth century. Such a spirit could hardly be on easy terms with the pope. He kept the peace by promising to lead a crusade, but had to postpone it because an epidemic decimated his army, and Gregory IX anathematized him. A year later Frederick set sail for the Near East. Setting greater store by words than the sword, through skilful diplomatic negotiations with the Saracens he obtained Jerusalem, Bethlehem and Nazareth without a fight; he then took for himself, without asking anyone for permission, the crown of the 'Christian Kingdom of Jerusalem'. He later effected a reconciliation with the pope, but his intellectual independence led to another dispute when he was proclaimed an anti-Christ. After him, such strong personalities no longer appeared in Germany. His sixteen-year-old grandson Conradin, the last of the Hohen-

38

38.   The Saar (French: Sarre), a tributary of the Mosel, rises near Lörchingen, at the confluence of the Red and White Saar. It is some 125 miles in length, but only its lower reaches are navigable.

39.   The Saar is linked to the Rhine-Main-Danube waterways system by a canal, used primarily for the transport of coal. The river has given its name to the entire region, Saarland, an area long disputed by France and Germany.

41

40, 41.   The Rhine, which the Germans in
their ancient poems called 'Daddy Rhine'
(Väterchen Rhein), is the country's biggest
river, though it rises in Switzerland and
empties into the sea in the Netherlands. In
its most scenic section, between Coblenz
and Mainz, the steep banks are dotted
with picturesque little towns, castles and
vineyards. Here, too, is the famous Lorelei
rock.

42

42. Bacharach in the Rhine gorge is also dominated by a formerly great fortress, Burg Stahleck. Its still impressive remains have been a youth hostel since the 1920s. This delightful town is often mentioned in literature: in poems by Victor Hugo, Ricarda Huch and others, and in Heinrich Heine's unfinished novel 'The Rabbi of Bacharach'. Heine wrote of the condition of German Jews in the late medieval period, approaching the topic with his characteristic irony and wit, satirizing the Jews and hence his own origins.

43

43.   The Mosel, too, has some quaint medieval towns along its banks. Of the fortress of Bernkastel, built c. 1000, only ruins remain. The town that grew up below it, now called Bernkastel-Kues, is known for its beautiful half-timbered houses and good wine. In the suburb of Kues is the late Gothic hospital of St Nicholas, endowed in the 15th century by the famous cardinal and philosopher Nicolaus von Kues (Cusanus), who stipulated that 33 local paupers could receive free board and lodging here.

44.   The medieval wine town of Oberwesel, on the Rhine just north of Bacharach, has many half-timbered houses characteristic of old German architecture. The construction of a storied building rests on a skeleton frame of crossed beams which remain exposed on the façade, the interstices filled with plaster and bricks.

45

45–47. *In such a setting it seems natural that girls should wear traditional costumes reminiscent of a more romantic past, or adaptations of these at carnival time when they parade through the town.*

47

48

48–50. Schönbusch ('beautiful bush') park near Aschaffenburg, is the oldest classically-landscaped park in Germany. Laid out in the 18th century for the electors of Mainz, it has a neoclassical 'pleasure house' (1779) and a number of pavilions in this charming setting. The town of Aschaffenburg is also known for its goldsmiths' guildhouse dated 1538, now housing a museum of applied arts, and the huge Schloss Johannisburg beside the Main. Built of red sandstone in the 17th century, it is the earliest Renaissance palace in Germany, and one of the most impressive.

49

50

52

51.   Einhardbasilika in Michelstadt, one of the best preserved buildings dating from the Carolingian era, was raised in the 9th century by Einhard, Charlemagne's biographer and overseer of his building work. It was originally intended to house the relics of St Marcellinus and St Peter, brought from Rome, but these were transferred to the nearby monastery of Seligenstadt, where Einhard died and was buried in 840.

52.   The interior of Maulbronn abbey church, founded in 1178. As legend has it, a group of monks, seeking a place to establish a new community, loaded their few belongings on a mule and let the animal decide. The mule stopped to drink at the source of the Hall, and it was here in the peaceful Salzach valley that they settled down in 1147. The spring still flows from a fountain in the garden of the abbey, formerly Cistercian but since 1538 a Lutheran-Evangelical seminary.

53

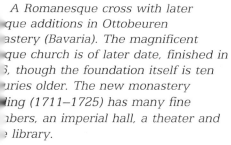

A Romanesque cross with later
que additions in Ottobeuren
astery (Bavaria). The magnificent
que church is of later date, finished in
, though the foundation itself is ten
uries older. The new monastery
ding (1711–1725) has many fine
bers, an imperial hall, a theater and
library.

Religious art from Ingolstadt. In the
le Ages this Bavarian town on the
be played an important part in the
ual and cultural life of the region, and
a center of the Counter-Reformation.
iversity was founded here in 1472.
ancient Bavarian craft of woodcarving
een placed in the service of the
ch since very early times.

54

63

55

55, 56.   The Residenz, Würzburg: the grand staircase and part of the fresco by Tiepolo on its vaulting. This huge palace of the prince bishops of Würzburg is the most famous example of south German Baroque, built between 1719 and 1744 by Balthasar Neumann, the greatest architect of his time. A Mozart festival is held every year in the imperial hall, one of the magnificent state rooms. Würzburg, among the most beautiful cities in all Germany, lies on the banks of the Main in northern Bavaria. Its bishops were made dukes of Franconia in the 12th century and it soon became a center of learning and the arts. Its university dates from 1582.

58

57, 58. The Benedictine monastery
church in Ottobeuren with its many
brilliantly colored frescoes and
a sculpturally ornamented organ is
considered a masterpiece of German
Baroque. The architect was J. M. Fischer
(1692–1766), and the frescoes are by
J. J. Zeiller. Characteristic of Fischer's work
is the way in which he fuses the variety of
decoration in the different parts of
a building into a harmonious architectural
whole.

63. Beyreuth: the Rococo interior of the Markgräfliches Opera House. (1745–48). It was the existence of this theater that attracted Richard Wagner to Beyreuth as a place to live and establich his festival. Later (1872–76), a much larger theater with 1900 seats was specially built for the Wagner festival, still held annually in this Bavarian town. ▷ ▷

60

59, 60. Tübingen: detail of the pulpit and view of tombs in the Protestant collegiate church of St George (1470–1500), an outstanding example of the late Gothic style. The choir has thirteen tombs of dukes of Württemberg, a gallery of local rulers that includes Eberhard the Bearded, who founded Tübingen University in 1477. The church is noted for its medieval carving and sculpture.

61

61. Library of the former Benedictine abbey of Amorbach, decorated in neoclassical style in the 18th century. The abbey was reputedly founded in 734, but most of the extensive monastery complex is 18th-century Baroque.

62. On the island of Herrenchiemsee in the Chiemsee, Bavaria's largest lake, King Ludwig II, after a visit to Versailles, decided to build 'something similar'. One of the most magnificent rooms is the Hall of Mirrors. ▷

63
64

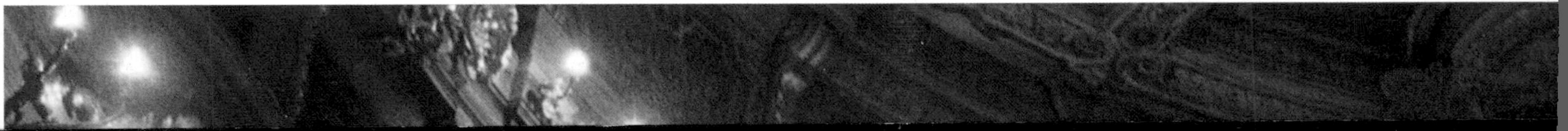

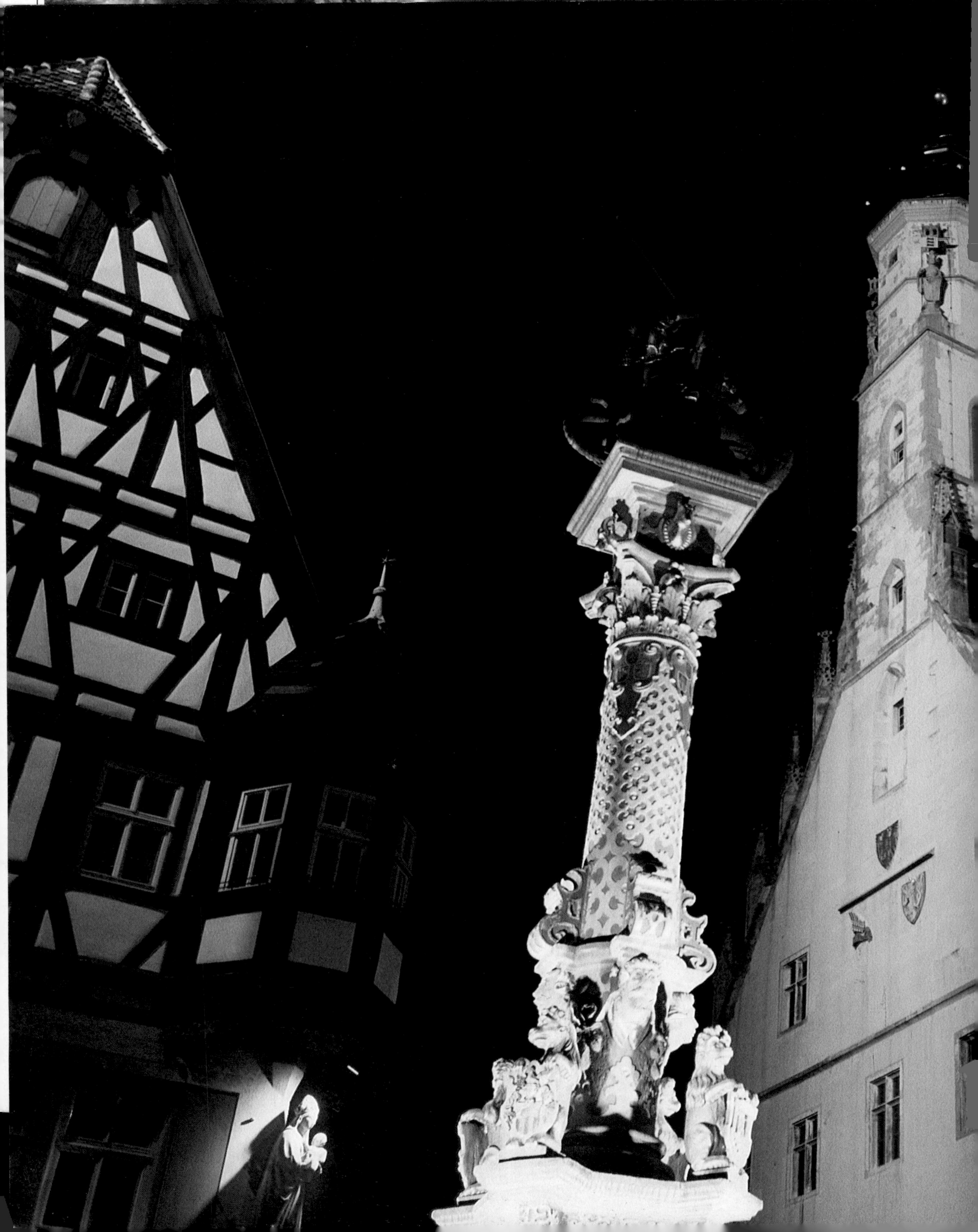

64, 65. Rothenburg on the Tauber (Bavaria) is unique in having preserved virtually unchanged the entire old town from the 14th to 17th centuries, with many buildings of exceptional charm. Not surprisingly, the principal livelihood here is tourism. Its attractions include the Rathaus (64), part 13th century (center) and part 16th century in date, with its old clock which at various hours summons the members of different guilds to have a drink. In front is the Georgbrunnen fountain (1608). Schmiedgasse (65) is one of several streets where time (unlike the clock) seems to have stood still.

66

66. Modern students in ancient Heidelberg, the small town on the Neckar which is the seat of the second oldest German university (after Prague), founded in 1386. Its former student life of duels, songs and romance, celebrated in operetta, seems to have vanished, but there is still a romantic air about the old town dominated by its huge Schloss. Here in Hauptstrasse stands the Gothic church of the Holy Spirit (right) with attractive small shops around its base.

67

67. Interior of Würzburg Cathedral (Dom St Kilian), fourth largest in Germany, which occupies an important place in German church architecture. Begun in 1045, it has retained its original Romanesque exterior and nave, but was given a Baroque choir and transept in the 18th century. Its interior is noted for its magnificent collection of carved tombs ranging from a period of over 700 years.

68. Shloss Rastatt, built between 1697 and 1705 as the residence of Margrave Ludwig Wilhelm of Baden, was the first large Baroque palace in Germany. The architect Rossi, following the ideas of the margrave and his wife, created an entire new planned town at Rastatt, with the huge Schloss as its focal point. Its sumptuous murals, sculpture, and stuccowork make it a masterpiece of the Baroque style. The Schloss now houses the Memorial Museum of Freedom Movements and German Military History Museum.

69. A Romanesque wall painting in the central apse of the church of SS Peter and Paul at Niederzell on the island of Reichenau in Germany's largest lake, Bodensee (Constance). Baroque frescoes and stuccowork were added much later to this ancient church dating from the 8th–9th century, when the monastery of Reichenau became a great center of learning and the arts.

70. Amorbach: ceiling frescoes by M. Gunther in the Benedictine abbey church of St. Mary. The Rococo interior decoration of this 18th-century church is among the finest in southern Germany.

staufen line, accompanied an army to Italy, but met with failure, and the young claimant to the imperial throne was beheaded in Naples.

The numerous petty states of Germany were governed by local rulers, bearing such titles as *Herzog, Erzherzog, Fürst*, sometimes merely *Graf*, while some were bishops combining spiritual and secular authority. Thanks to the growth of trade, a burgeoning middle class and a better grasp of finance and commerce, certain communities managed to obtain the status of 'imperial free city' *(Freie Reichstadt)*. The most prosperous in the north formed a commercial association known as the Hanseatic League; the Hansa towns *(Hansastadt)* were actually the first republics in northern Europe. From the thirteenth century on, the leader was the Baltic port of Lübeck (much later to be known as the birthplace of Thomas Mann, who immortalized it in his novel *Buddenbrooks*).

Riding across Germany, robber barons *(Raubritter)* with their bands pillaged and plundered the land, stashing their booty in hilltop castles. These fantastic, inaccessible fortifications are much admired today, with no thought given to their use as brigand strongholds. Insecurity and lawlessness prevailed throughout the land, yet the emperor was still formally elected ruler of the Holy Roman Empire (so named from 1157). Those entitled to vote for the emperor, the electoral princes, preferred weak rulers, so they could continue to do as they pleased. In 1273 they misjudged their man, picking a little-known count from the territory of present-day Switzerland. His family name is said to have been taken from the castle of Habsburg (Hawk's Castle). *Nomen est omen* – the Habsburgs demonstrated a hawk-like capacity for extending their dominions. Though Rhinelanders by origin – the castle of Habsburg stood beside the Aar, a tributary of the Rhine – all their more important estates were on the territory of present-day Austria. Rudolf Habsburg, having become German emperor, acquired Alsace and Swabia, and only then established himself in the Austrian provinces of Carinthia, Styria and Carniola. Following his victory over the Bohemian king, Otokar, he pursued a policy of aggrandizement based on marriage settlements. This was to become an Austrian tradition. Years later people would say that while the rest of the world went to war, lucky Austria got what it wanted simply by getting married.

The German princes and dukes, bishops and towns, soon began to fear this dynasty, and for the next century and a half elected other, less well-known nobles as their rulers. Outstanding among them was Charles IV of Luxembourg, who transferred the German capital to the Bohemian city of Prague, founding there the first German university. In 1356 he promulgated the Golden Bull, the basic law of the empire *(Reichsgrundgesetz)*, which conferred the election of the emperor upon seven electors. These were the archbishops of Cologne, Mainz and Trier, the count palatine *(Pfalzgraf)* of the Rhine, the king of Bohemia, the duke of Saxony-Wittenberg and the margrave of Brandenburg. What is most important, they declared papal approval to be no longer necessary. Through the bishops the pope had the possibility of influencing three votes, but in this matter the German bishops were not particularly obedient to their spiritual leader in Rome. The electors chose the Holy Roman Emperor of the German Nation, as he was now styled. The authority of the electors, except of course the three archbishops, was hereditary; the emperor's was not. But this did not worry the Habsburgs. After 1438 they simply appropriated the imperial crown, which did not guarantee them special

The Rise of the Habsburgs

71.   The 12th-century church of the Cistercian monastery of Maulbronn. The order had monasteries throughout Germany, France and England, all built in the same ascetically simple style, without ornamentation. The later painted net vaulting seen here is not in keeping with the general austerity. After the Reformation in Germany and the Revolution in France the order declined, and its church buildings were often taken over by the Protestants, as happened at Maulbronn.

privileges but sounded good. Their possessions in the German-speaking south continued to expand, and Austria grew into a powerful nation, uniting numerous non-Germanic people – Slav, Italian and Hungarian.

While most of the peoples of Europe were developing their nation states, Germany continued to fragment into petty principalities. The Austrians and Bavarians may have been very similar, but their two ambitious dynasties, the Habsburgs and the Wittelbachs, kept them apart. It should be mentioned that several smaller Germanic peoples – the Dutch, for example, or the Swiss – steered an independent course, away from Germany, though this could not have been predicted during the Middle Ages. In this connection it is hard to perceive any logic in history. In the Middle Ages, comparatively strong alliances of states centered on Lombardy and the Rhine seemed feasible. Yet these ideas vanished without a trace. In contrast, the freedom-loving farmers living around the Vierwaldstätter (a lovely name meaning a lake near four forests), in the cantons of Uri, Shwyz and Unterwald, entered into their 'eternal league' *(Ewige Bund)* in resistance to Habsburg oppression. Its date, 1291, is usually considered the beginning of the Swiss confederation. The peasants' pledge proved so firm that Switzerland never entered a union with the German states, retaining its independence and individuality to this day.

Many factors played a part in the further development of Germany. During the Middle Ages the Christian city of Cologne was just as important as Paris, but the French and their dynasty steadily gained power. The Slavs in the east followed their own designs. The German kings seemed to be perpetually in a state of war in Italy and over Italy, either seeking the pope's clemency and blessing, or opposing his secular influence. Largely because of this, the Italians also failed to unite for a long time.

Germany's North Sea coast is comparatively short, and sailing out of the Baltic is hazardous, so the Germans never managed to establish close maritime links with other continents, unlike the British, Spanish, Portuguese, even the Dutch. Lacking a united state and a large fleet, they never became world traders, and were too late to secure for themselves a slice of the colonial cake. The fact that Germany remained a collection of continental states also influenced the way its inhabitants viewed the rest of the world.

The Reformation

A German Jew, Karl Marx, would later remark ironically that even in the Christian Middle Ages a man could not live from religion alone. The Church, however, prescribed people's conduct, how they lived, and their economic and esthetic standards.

In the early sixteenth century, church authorities in Rome decided to raise a magnificent cathedral on the site of the old church of St. Peter's. To obtain funds, the pope resorted to the long-established practice of selling indulgences. Originally this had been commutation for money of part of the temporal penance due for sins, but as time passed, authorized indulgence sellers made more extravagant claims: the purchase of indulgences could reduce the time spent in purgatory. Opposition to this practice had long been growing among churchmen, even before the pope's authorization of special indulgences for the rebuilding of St. Peter's. The Dominican Johann Tetzel, who was entrusted with the fund-raising drive in Germany, went so far as to claim that anyone who contributed enough money would not have to appear at the Last Judgment.

In Wittenburg, capital of Frederick the Wise, ruler of Saxony, the sale of indulgences aroused the indignation of a German Augustinian friar and professor of theology, Martin Luther. As an invitation to debate, he nailed his 95 theses on the inadmissibility of this practice on the door of the castle church. His act stands as a landmark in the history of Christendom, and also precipitated a war more devastating to Germany than any other before or after.

In 1517, when Luther rebelled against the greatest spiritual and temporal power of the age, he was thirty-four years old. At first his theses could be understood as grounds for a lively theological debate. It certainly did not enter his mind to attack the papacy or the Church as a whole. He wanted only to correct what he felt were obvious errors and abuses. Salvation, he declared, could not be purchased; the divine gift of grace was freely given to all those who lived by faith. The pope had no jurisdiction over purgatory, so the vendors of papal indulgences were deceiving the people. At first Pope Leo X did not take the attack very seriously; he sent Cardinal Cajetan to persuade Luther to recant. The stubborn friar refused. In 1519, as the polemic became more acrimonious, he went a step further and declared, "The pope in Rome has no right to take new stands as regards faith . . . Nor can a pious Christian be obliged to accept anything but what is written in Holy Scripture." The pope condemned and then excommunicated him.

Title page of one of Luther's tracts from 1521 showing a printer at work.

The son of a Saxon miner who had become a prosperous entrepreneur, Luther received a good education, but abandoned his law studies and the prospect of a lucrative career to enter a monastery. Familiar with the hard life and tribulations of the common man, he remarked that every year Germany sent about half a million guldens to Rome, ". . . and after this it surprises us that the nobles, cities, villages, people, are growing poorer. We ought to be surprised that we still have anything left to eat!" This naturally appealed to the rulers of the small German states, who were reluctant to recognize the pope's spiritual authority or contribute money for his architectural projects. At the imperial diet convened at Worms in 1521 they induced Charles V, the newly elected Holy Roman Emperor, to summon Luther to speak before them, and to guarantee the recalcitrant friar safe-conduct. On this occasion Luther, visibly moved, vigorously delivered before the assembly of nobles his famous words, "I neither can nor will recant anything, since it is neither right nor safe to act against conscience. God help me. Amen."

The emperor kept his word and let him go free, but a month later issued the Edict of Worms, declaring Luther an outlaw, which meant that anyone could kill him with impunity. Unwittingly the emperor had permanently divided the German nobility. Anxious for his safety, Luther's patron, Elector Frederick of Saxony, had him taken to the Wartburg castle. There, in peace and seclusion, the learned doctor of divinity undertook to translate the New Testament from the original Greek, beginning in fact his work on fixing the standard of the German language. Peasant revolts soon broke out throughout the land, especially in the south and southwest, the rebels citing Luther's words, "According to the Bible we are all free men!"

Historian Golo Mann describes the situation as follows; "In Germany the nation was nearly split in half by the religious quarrels of the sixteenth century. This split did not happen elsewhere . . . Protestantism was originally a German affair. It was born in Germany and there — to use an

abused expression since we have no other – it became a popular movement within a few years. In Germany Protestantism found its incarnation in a man unique among the spiritual leaders of the day, not because of the power of his mind – in that respect Calvin was superior to Luther – but because of his popularity, his magnetic strength and depth of character. Why was Martin Luther, the poet and writer, the mystic, the inspiring preacher, the born politician and demagogue, unable to give the nation new spiritual and temporal unity, why did he fail to achieve what a few clever English rulers accomplished without much difficulty? The problems that faced Luther were too hopelessly entangled; he could not unravel them.''

It was naturally the concern of the emperor to retain control over as much as possible of his vast realms. Moreover, he was a strongly religious man, dedicated to preserving the unity of the Church. But Charles V had much else to occupy his mind beside the spread of the Lutheran cause in Germany. He had inherited Spain as well as Austria, Burgundy and the Netherlands. In his long reign, he fought the Turks, warred with France, campaigned in North Africa, while his conquistadors in Mexico and Peru laid the foundations of the Spanish colonial empire. For these reasons he did not take too seriously a little unpleasantness in Germany, though in the end his failure to suppress Protestantism and preserve church unity must have contributed to his decision to abdicate, and retire to the solitude of a Spanish monastery in 1556.

Luther's sermons and writings not only met with the approval of the independent-minded German princes and cities, but also sparked off rebellion among the long-suffering peasantry. As long as it was directed against the emperor, this suited the rulers, but when their own privileges were questioned and the risings assumed an alarming scale, they demanded that Luther bring his followers to their senses. Luther complied, vehemently denouncing any form of violence, thus distancing himself from the serfs and their demands for liberty. The division in the Church, however, was irreversible. From attacking indulgences, Luther had gone on to preach far-reaching reform of the Church's rites and practices: the use of the vernacular in services, the reduction of the seven sacraments to two – Baptism and Communion, the abolition of celibacy of the clergy. (He himself married a former nun, Katherine von Bora, in 1525, a union that proved long and happy.) All these reforms were soon adopted by the German states and cities that supported Luther and were known as the 'Protesting Estates' – hence the name Protestant.

The split in the Church deepened as the Evangelicals distanced themselves from the Roman Catholic community. Europe's rulers took advantage of the situation as it suited them politically. Henry VIII of England, for example, had defended the papacy against Luther and received the title 'defender of the faith', but when the pope refused to grant him a divorce, he retaliated like the German theologian and broke off ties with Rome, establishing the Anglican Church with himself as supreme head.

As it turned out, Luther's words were just as explosive as the invention of another German monk, Berthold Schwarz, who several centuries earlier had discovered a kind of powder that now came into general use for military purposes. In the mid-fifteenth century another German of historical importance, Johannes Gensfleisch, better known as Gutenberg, invented a way to reproduce the written word by means of movable lead type. This skill, already nearly a hundred years old, was also perfected during Luther's time. Thus, two German inventions connected with lead – printing and gunpowder – were instrumental in the spread of Luther's teachings and their consequences. Without printed books the new ideas would not have spread so quickly; without gunpowder to project lead shot the struggles between Protestants and Catholics would never have been so bloody.

At his last diet convened in Augsburg in 1555, Charles V was reluctantly obliged to recognize the Lutherans and renounce the idea of uniformity of creed in the empire. The rulers of the German states thereupon reached a decision typical of their time: the sovereign's confession would be obligatory for all his subjects. If a prince became a Lutheran, all the inhabitants of his country would do likewise; if he opted for Catholicism, so would his subjects. An individual's personal convictions were immaterial. However, this Peace of Augsburg did not extend toleration to the other forms of Protestantism that had sprung up.

Luther was no longer among the living when this happened and could not comment. For Germany a divided Church meant an even greater rift in the union that still held the German states together. In 1608 the Protestant rulers formally organized their own union; a year later the Catholic rulers joined the Catholic League. Of course, it was not by chance that the Protestants were mostly in the north, and the Catholics largely in the south and southwest of Germany. This simply confirmed the line of demarcation which, as we have seen, had long existed.

The Thirty Years' War

Until the early seventeenth century Germany had passed through more or less the same stages as the rest of western Europe: the rule of ancient Rome, conversion to Christianity, feudalism and the Crusades. Cathedrals, monasteries and universities were built, towns developed with their social classes, crafts and commerce. Now, however, Germany began to take a different path. Preoccupied with itself, it did not send out expeditions to other continents. The British, Spanish, Dutch, Portuguese and French carried their flags to distant lands. Throughout this whole period the German princes would occasionally grab a sleepy provincial town from one another. When the great Anglo-Saxon colonization of North America began, the Thirty Years' War broke out, in 1618, completely devastating Germany. A contemporary historian noted, "Of all the great wars of recent times, the Thirty Years' War was the most insane."

This complex religious and political struggle – in fact a series of wars – was initially provoked by a conflict of interests within the German empire, though all the other great powers of the period intervened, particularly France and Sweden. In this war of Catholics against Protestants, Bavaria naturally sided with the Catholics and the Habsburgs of Austria, but was soon obliged to oppose the latter's encroachments, for the Habsburg empire included Spain; Bavaria had to consider the interests of Germany as a whole and thus found itself in league with the Protestant states. French intervention was directed against the Habsburgs and not against Germany, though the French crown was Catholic, just like the Austrian. Sweden defended first and foremost its supremacy on the Baltic

'The Crucifixion' by Albrecht Dürer, woodcut, c. 1497.

Sea, and even though it was a leading Protestant country, it turned against the north German Protestant states, its neighbors, and found itself on the side of Catholicism. In the end, few knew who was fighting whom and why.

Appearing in the midst of this turmoil was a wealthy landowner from Bohemia who, despite his fine-sounding German name, preferred to correspond in Czech. This high-class soldier of fortune and resourceful military commander was Wallenstein.

Emperor Rufolf II had guaranteed Protestant Bohemia religious freedom, and it was not inclined to recognize as its next ruler a fervent champion of the Counter-Reformation, Rudolf's cousin, Ferdinand of Styria, later Emperor Ferdinand II, who . had already forcibly recatholicized inner Austria. It all began with an apparently insignificant incident. Protestant nobles of Bohemia had come to Hradcany castle in Prague, then the residence of the German sovereign, to lodge complaints with the imperial governors, counts Martinitz and Slavat, but quarreled so violently they threw the governors out of the windows along with their secretary, Fabricius. Falling from a considerable height, the lords fortunately landed in a moat filled with mud and excrement, which saved their lives. Nevertheless, this was the signal for an insurrection that turned Germany for thirty years into a battleground mercilessly ravaged by mercenary armies. Villages and towns were put to the torch, livestock and harvests were destroyed; between 1618 and 1648 Germany lost a third of its population.

Countless works of literature have been inspired by the Thirty Years' War. Friedrich Schiller wrote a dramatic trilogy with Wallenstein as the central figure, and also a scholarly *History of the Thirty Years' War.* Chronicling the horrors of the period, Bertolt Brecht's best-known play *Mother Courage,* shows that the 'small man' can sometimes find a way to profit during wartime but inevitably loses out in the end.

History records primarily the names of the powerful. We know of Bavarian Count Tilly, Evangelical Duke Bernhard of Weimar, and above all the imperial generalissimo, Albrecht von Wallenstein. The strings in Germany were pulled by such potentates as Swedish King Gustavus Adolphus, Danish King Christian, French statesman Cardinal Richelieu. All the while, Germany's peasants were being slaughtered or dying of starvation. In 1648, when the Peace of Westphalia was finally concluded, the German empire, hitherto largely a fiction, no longer existed.

Prussia Grows Strong

Amid the most abject misery new leaders often emerge, sparks spring from embers, kindling a new flame. Born in 1620 after the beginning of the Thirty Years' War, an impoverished young aristocrat set about restoring a German province around which others would later assemble. This was Frederick William (Friedrich Wilhelm), in historical accounts known as the Great Elector. At the age of twenty he was so poor he had to borrow fifteen thalers from a Berlin magistrate in order to support his household. At the age of fifty he was sometimes ally, sometimes opponent, but in any case a match for the French Sun King, Louis XIV. A fervent Calvinist with a strong belief in his religious mission as ruler, he turned his homeland, Brandenburg and Pomerania, into a Protestant state that would form the nucleus of the future Prussia. Descended from the old, though at the time not too illustrious, family of Hohenzollern, Frederick William managed to consolidate his position on

72. *Windmills near the town of Kappeln in the northern province of Schleswig-Holstein are reminiscent of olden times, but may soon have scores of brand-new neighbors. As the need for clean sources of energy grows, new designs for electricity-generating windmills are being tested, particularly near the North Sea.*

73. *Holland is generally considered the land of flowers, but if statistics existed, the Germans would probably take a close second place to the Dutch as flower fanciers. Public parks, private gardens and balconies are a blaze of color for much of the year. ▷*

the ruins of the Thirty Years' War, making political capital for his heirs, who would head the revived German empire some two hundred years later.

Frederick William excelled in civil and military administration. In a sense he was the creator of modern state organization. Before his time rulers and military commanders had engaged mercenaries for every campaign, for the season, as it were. Frederick William set up a regular, professional army, the first in modern Europe. From civil servants he demanded the same discipline as from his soldiers and officers. He formed the first cabinet in the modern sense; namely, the members of his 'secret council' were assigned departments for which they were responsible. Supervision was his own prerogative: he opened and read every letter personally, then forwarded it to the appropriate department and associates for action. Undertaking economic reforms based on his own ideas, he developed a fixed system of direct and indirect taxation and levied duties to protect his country's fledgling textile industry. Realizing that the potato, imported from America, could solve the problem of nourishing the population, he had this crop planted on experimental fields. Henceforth, no one would ever have to die of starvation in Germany. The state flourished, but he needed more people, more subjects. He declared, "For me people are the greatest wealth." In a shrewd move, he encouraged the immigration of 20,000 French Protestants, Huguenots as they were called, persecuted by the Catholics. Naturally he was not motivated by pure humanitarianism or sympathy for fellow Protestants; many were well-to-do and educated, bringing with them capital and knowledge of various trades. Their descendants were to play an important role in Germany, becoming good, perhaps the best, Germans, only recognizable by their French surnames. The first freely elected premier of East Germany in 1990 was Lothar de Maizière. At the same time the Social Democratic candidate for West German prime minister was Oskar Lafontaine.

Prussia took its name from the Old Prussians (Prusi or Borussi), a Baltic people converted to Christianity by the Teutonic Knights. These Prussians, who lived near the Weichsel and Niemen rivers, had little impact on the state to which they gave their name. Prussia existed as a state, in fact, only about one hundred and fifty years. Today, the Germans themselves find the word prejudicial. An old French dictionary reads: "Prussia, a kingdom created through wars and pillaging expeditions." In the eighteenth century Count Mirabeau, the French statesman, wrote: "Other states have an army; in Prussia the army has a state."

All this is quite untrue: Prussia was never run by a bloodthirsty military corps. On the contrary, its soldiers were disciplined and orderly, the officers paid less than elsewhere and strictly forbidden to dabble in politics. Prussian kings were for the most part diligent, frugal, occasionally avaricious, but at the expense of their favorite plaything – the army. At an early stage Prussia was a state governed by law. In civil disputes the king was a party like any other, and sometimes lost his suit.

The first king of Prussia, Frederick (Friedrich) I of the Hohenzollern family, crowned himself. During the ceremony the court pastor stated that "All regents in the world are there because of their subjects, not the subjects because of their rulers." His son and heir, Frederick William (Friedrich Wilhelm) I, assuming power in 1713, first sold his father's ermine coronation robe, its diamond clips earning him 30,000 ducats, and ordered all the silver plate in his palaces to be melted down to pay off the state debts. He dismissed most of the courtiers and personally assumed

78–80. A ruined castle near Bad Dürkheim (Rhineland Palatinate). The first-time visitor to Germany is always astonished by the number of fortifications and castles – a relic of the time when every small area had its feudal lord. Many of the castles are still habitable, used as homes or as museums or hotels.

79

80

81. The Baroque town hall of Bonn, built in the 18th century. Until selected as the capital of the Federal Republic, the town was a popular place for a quiet retirement. Many new buildings have sprung up for the needs of the government and parliament, but the old town hall is still the mayor's office, where visiting heads of state call to sign the gold visitors' book.

82. A few souvenirs from a more belligerant era also remain in Bonn. An ancient cannon still stands in front of the old customs house, guarding the town's independence since the devastating wars of the 17th century.

83

83. Bonn University with its prestigious liberal arts and medical schools was founded in 1818. The rector's office and assembly halls are still housed in the Baroque former electoral palace, where the young and unknown Ludwig van Beethoven gave his first concerts. His father was the bishop's vintner. Beethoven's birthplace, close to the palace, is one of the city's chief tourist attractions.

85

85. The old opera house in Frankfurt has now been renovated for concerts and special entertainments. Operas are performed in a new theater, actually three theaters in one sharing a common foyer. The headquarters of Germany's major banks, Frankfurt allocates more per capita for the arts than any other city in the world.

84. This fountain with its female figure in front of Frankfurt town hall reminds passerslay that if necessary justice, symbolized by the scales is her left hand, will be meted aut by the sword.

86

86. Goethe Square in Frankfurt. Germany's greatest poet was born in 1749 in this city. Characteristic of Frankfurt is its skyline of highrise buildings raised by the big banks and insurance companies, producing a juxtapostion of old monuments and ultra-modern façades.

87. The casino café in Baden-Baden. As the word baden means to bathe, it is hard to think of a more appropriate name for a spa. Its hyphenated name in fact refers to the town of Baden in the principality of Baden. Today the province is called Baden-Württemberg, i. e. the principality of Baden and the old kingdom of Württemberg.

88

88. The promenade in the old part of Baden-Baden, with the casino in the background. Thanks to its situation amid thick forests but not far from population centers, combined with its pleasant mild climate, luxurious facilities and, above all, its alkali, radioactive and salt springs, this is the most frequented spa in a country where 'taking the waters' is still very popular.

89. Baden-Baden was a spa in Roman times. The hot springs rising from a depth of 6600 feet were already in use then. Beneath present-day Roman Square (Römerplatz) are the ruins of baths where Roman legionaries would soak out the aches from long marches.

89

90

90.   The spit of land at the confluence of
the Rhine and Mosel near the city of
Coblenz is called Deutsches Eck (German
corner), and is considered by some to be
the heart of Germany. The large
equestrian statue of Kaiser Wilhelm which
once stood here was badly damaged in
1945 and only the plinth remains, as
a monument to German unity.

91.   Young Germans look much like their
contemporaries elsewhere in the West.
One may have a way-out haircut, another
an American-style T-shirt, and the
conversation by the lake near Berlingen
may well be about similar topics – pop
music, girls and sport.

92. An unusual statue in Coblenz, suggestive of the peddlars of yore who traveled around selling their goods from a bag or tray. Like many other German towns, ancient Coblenz has decorated its newly-created pedestrian zones with attractive, often amusing figures.

91

the duties of field marshal, i.e. commander-in-chief of the army, and minister of finance, so as to control these vital functions and also save on salaries. Then he increased the size of the army. From his father he had inherited 38,000 soldiers; when he died in 1740, his army numbered 83,000 domestic recruits and foreign mercenaries.

Frederick William governed sternly and treated his family rather sadistically. After working sixteen hours a day, only in the evening would he allow himself a pipe of tobacco and a glass of beer. He particularly maltreated his son. Somewhat effeminate by nature, young Frederick initially hated the army. His first love, a certain Countess Orcelska, invariably appeared dressed in male attire. The young prince tried to flee from Germany with the aid of his instructor and close, perhaps too close, friend, Lieutenant Katte. The fugitives were caught, and the king compelled the unfortunate prince to watch his friend's execution through the window of his prison cell at Küstrin castle.

This stern upbringing produced results. On ascending the throne, Frederick II turned out to be an excellent military leader. Victorious in wars against Austria and Russia, he secured territorial gains for Prussia and entered history as Frederick the Great. Remembered is his famous rallying call to his soldiers, hesitating before a charge, "What is it, lads, do you want to live forever?"

Frederick the Great was a complex personality. Dutifully, he married the proper princess, though it was widely known that he did not care for women. He became one of Germany's most outstanding rulers, yet considered the German language vulgar – in his proximity only French was spoken. He conducted himself as an absolute monarch, yet invited the free-thinking Voltaire to his court, preferring his company to all others. His qualities as a commander are generally recognized, yet he wrote lyrical poems and played the flute. He gave his lovely new *château* at Potsdam the French name of Sans Souci. The last foreign visitor he received was Mirabeau.

At the age of seventy he wrote, "If someone improves his land, drains swamps and in that way gains fertile new land, he becomes a conqueror but without barbarism." He was so fond of his dogs that when they died he had them buried under marble tombstones. After one of his military victories he said, "Fame is vanity. Do men deserve any praise at all? They are celebrated only for causing a commotion."

Frederick the Great marked an era, not only in Germany but in Europe as well, the period ending with the French Revolution. He died in 1786. Though he did not become master of all Germany, he was no longer simply one of numerous petty rulers. He waged three wars, which cost him half a million soldiers and 150 million thalers. He defeated the Austrians, Russians, French and a host of other German sovereigns. Several times he was on the verge of disaster. When the Russians had already overrun a large part of Prussia, he was saved by the death of Empress Elizabeth. He made Prussia the fifth great power, alongside Britain, France, Russia and Austria, and a nucleus for the unification of all Germans.

Revolutionary Times

During the crises precipitated by the French Revolution and Napoleon's campaigns, Germany remained fairly passive. Golo Mann says, "The storm blew elsewhere. Germany only felt its effects." True, Austria tried, together with Prussia, hitherto its enemy, to intervene against the

Der Hessische Landvote.
Erste Botschaft.

Portrait of Georg Büchner (1813–1837) on the title-page of his revolutionary pamphlet: 'Der hessische Landbote' (1834).

revolution, but Prussia soon withdrew, more preoccupied with a new partition of Poland it was negotiating with Russia, and abandoned the entire west bank of the Rhine to France.

Goethe, the greatest German poet of all time, is supposed to have said after the battle at Valmy on September 20, 1792, "In this place and on this day a new epoch is beginning and you can all say that you witnessed it." This sounds good, but it is only legend. Goethe did accompany his patron, Charles Augustus (Karl August), Duke of Weimar, commander of the 6th Regiment of Cuirassiers, but in his *Campaign in France*, written years later, we find no indication that he grasped the significance of this historic turning-point. The German attitude towards the turmoil in France can perhaps be described as follows: They've killed their king? Terrible! They're guillotining one another? No more than they deserve!

Later Goethe actually met Napoleon. Each of them, in his own way, was much too conscious of his own greatness. It was Napoleon who insisted on the meeting, receiving the poet at breakfast. Goethe was sixty years old, Napoleon twenty years younger. Goethe's greeting is well-known, "*Voilà un homme!*", which could have meant anything, though definitely intended as a compliment. Napoleon immediately said that he had read *Werther*, Goethe's first novel, seven times – flattering for any writer – and they discussed the theme of jealousy treated in this book. Finally the emperor came to the point and asked Goethe to write a play about him, suggesting that Goethe should move to Paris. He invited him the same evening to a gala theater performance to meet the Russian tsar. The Russian delegation included a Count Tolstoy, who later described the event to a relative – the author of *War and Peace*.

At a ball in Weimar the emperor repeated the invitation that Goethe should become 'his Corneille'. Napoleon then set out on his Russian campaign, against the very same tsar who had been his guest. Much later, retreating in haste, he happened to stop at Weimar and remembered to instruct someone, "Give my greetings to Monsieur Göta or whatever his name is..."

Napoleonic France was defeated by Russia, Britain and Austria. The contribution of the German states to the victory was sufficient to place them on the winning side but not enough to entitle them to dictate conditions in Europe. Napoleon had re-drawn the political map of Germany, and now the question of its future organization arose. In 1815, at the Congress of Vienna, a German union *(Deutscher Bund)* was formed. Conceived as a replacement for the former empire, it was joined by 39 sovereign states of various size: one empire (Austria), five kingdoms, numerous principalities and duchies, and four free city-republics: Lübeck, Frankfurt, Bremen and Hamburg.

This fact is often forgotten. Until the end of the nineteenth century Germany as a united state did not exist. What bound the Germans together was a common language, a common culture underlying a growing feeling of belonging together, and a desire for political unification. Though several of the German dynasties had emerged from the Napoleonic wars with the aura of victor, these pan-Germanic aspirations were generally directed against them, for progressive-minded Germans saw unification as a way to put an end to feudalism. The kings and princes therefore tried to suppress all new movements, newspapers were strictly censored, the universities were viewed with suspicion.

As elsewhere in Europe, 1848, the Year of Revolution, set off an explosion in Germany. The first national parliament met in St. Paul's

Church in Frankfurt on Main. As unity could not be imagined without some kind of dynastic formula, King Frederick William IV was offered the crown of a united German empire. Too much a conservative to accept the imperial throne from a popularly elected national assembly, he refused in disgust. "This would be a crown baked of rubbish and disloyalty, of broken pledges and high treason, a sausage roll from the butcher and the baker, not from the grace of God," declared the arrogant Prussian monarch.

Ironically, two of his subjects in the Rhine province (acquired by Prussia in 1815) were to play a major role in the ultimate destruction of the old order in Europe. They were a philosopher and writer, Dr. Karl Marx, and businessman Friedrich Engels, co-authors of the *Communist Manifesto,* which they published in Brussels in 1848. Though they were obliged to flee repressive Germany to settle permanently in more liberal England in 1849, it should not be forgetten that the idea of Communism was born beside the Rhine. It was a German idea.

Bismarck, Architect of the Empire

Succeeding the mentally deranged Frederick William IV, his brother William (Wilhelm) I ascended the Prussian throne in 1861. A year later he appointed as prime minister a man who would effect radical changes in Germany, Otto von Bismarck. Count Bismarck promised to solve the 'German question' with the aid of 'blood and iron'.

In Prussia, the struggle between king and parliament was already evident. In internal as well as foreign affairs, Bismarck displayed consummate skill, even negotiating with Marx's friend and representative in Germany, lawyer Ferdinand Lassalle, founder of the German Workers' Union, later the Social Democratic Party. Bismarck cultivated friendly relations with Russia, expanded Prussian territory at the expense of Denmark, and in 1866 defeated Austria, which had formed a confederation with the south Germans and several central German states. Bismarck then formed the North German Confederation, clearly aspiring to create a large, united Germany. French Emperor Napoleon III, perceiving danger for his own country, tried to prevent this development but was defeated by Prussia in the war of 1870/71. The war ended with the coronation of the Prussian king as 'German Emperor' in the palace of Versailles near Paris.

Bismarck seems to have desired the German empire more than the aged William. But to achieve this goal, it was not enough to defeat France; he had to win the approval of the other German sovereigns. In doing so, Bismarck resorted to cunning, concessions, bribes, all the legal and illegal means at his disposal. Especially important was the agreement of the Bavarian king, Ludwig II, constantly beset with financial problems. An extravagant builder of castles and patron of artists, particularly the composer Richard Wagner and his costly operas, he lived only for esthetic pleasures. And his fondness for boys. (Amorous entanglements were nothing new for the Bavarian court: his grandfather, Ludwig I, had been forced to abdicate because of his affair with the dancer Lola Montez.) Therefore, to obtain his consent, Bismarck promised Ludwig II a life-long annual allowance of 300,000 marks in gold, raising the money by confiscating the property of the exiled Hanoverian dynasty. For this allowance Ludwig signed a letter which William I and Bismarck could use in negotiations with other German kings and princes.

By that time already seventy-three years old, William I hesitated about accepting the honor until the very evening before his coronation. He complained, "As a king I was my own master, as emperor I have to do what others tell me." Moreover, the title was not 'Emperor of Germany' as he wished, but 'German Emperor', which he considered less exalted.

Germany was finally a united state, but *pro forma* more than in reality. Austria, of course, did not join Bismarck's creation and thus — at the end of the last century — ceased to be a German state.

Unlike the earlier German confederation which had included 39 entities, the German empire *(Deutsches Reich)* comprised 25 states, all retaining their previous internal organization. Among them were four kingdoms: Prussia, Bavaria, Saxony and Württemberg, 18 duchies and principalities, and three Hanseatic towns: Lübeck, Bremen and Hamburg. The discrepancy in numbers did not result from 14 states remaining outside the empire; certain frontiers had been revised, some of the smaller states no longer existed, the free city of Frankfurt, for example, had lost its autonomy, etc. True, the Prussian kings were now German emperors as well, and this was an hereditary title; likewise, the Prussian prime minister was 'chancellor of the *Reich*'; Prussian subjects comprised almost three-fifths of the population of the whole empire; yet the legal situation was highly complex, varying from state to state. The joint parliament *(Reichstag)* had only specified rights; the rights of the emperor — as old William had complained on assuming office — remained constitutionally undefined. Bismarck, as imperial chancellor, the real administrator of this large, newly-formed imperial confederation, relied more on his energy, prestige, and skill in manipulating people than on clearly delegated powers.

On the one hand, it was a period of economic prosperity and rapid industrialization; toward the end of the nineteenth century Germany boasted about 30,000 millionaires. Huge companies like the Krupp mines and steel mills and the Siemens electrical manufacturing works became bywords for quality throughout the world. In 1870 Germany produced

The reactionary victory in Europe, 1849, sketch by F. Schroeder in the 'Düsseldorf Monthly'.

only about one fifth as much iron as Great Britain; by the end of the century continental Germany matched the island country in the output of that strategic commodity, a yardstick of industrial might. In the three decades following the foundation of the *Reich* nearly 6,000 new corporations sprang up. Yet the German laborer worked twelve hours a day, seven days a week, without social security or holidays. The poverty in working-class families was such that children often had to work, too.

German historians call 1888 the 'year of three emperors'. Namely, the death of William I at the age of ninety-one was followed only ninety-nine days later by that of his son and heir Frederick II, and the succession of his twenty-nine-year-old grandson William II, better known as Kaiser Wilhelm.

The Last Emperor

William II was an arrogant young man, fond of boasting: "I decide policy!" At first in his speeches he promised improvements to the workers, sent telegrams to company owners instructing them to raise wages, hoping in this way to differentiate himself from his prime minister, Bismarck, whom he feared. In intimate circles the emperor would say, "For me every Social Democrat is an enemy of the fatherland." Two such headstrong personalities as Bismarck and William II could never work together, and the elderly chancellor was forced to resign in 1890. A famous British cartoon of the period depicts Germany as a large ship, William a comic figure standing on the bridge as Bismarck descends the gangway, with the caption: 'Dropping the pilot.'

Now the emperor was free to devote himself to parties, hunting and eccentric fancy-dress balls, from which women were excluded. He treated the army, and particularly the navy, as if they existed for his personal amusement. In 1902 he celebrated his 50,000th hunting trophy. Of all the positive qualities displayed by his ancestors: diligence, self-discipline, frugality and moderation, interest in the arts and artists, philosophers and writers, William inherited nothing.

By that time, though, Germany had become so rich and powerful that inept rule was not immediately felt. The Germans considered their share of the globe inadequate, likewise the presence of their fleet on the high seas, and in this respect public opinion coincided with the emperor's ambitions. It annoyed the Germans that their colonial possessions, particularly in Africa, were so modest compared to the British. Yet they had no idea how to remedy the situation; whatever they attempted turned out to be too late. Their abortive efforts to gain access to China and other spots in the Far East had been ill-advised. More promising was a project to finance the building of a railroad to Baghdad leading across the Balkan peninsula. It was supposed eventually to link Berlin with Teheran. Here there was a bit more logic, at least from the point of view of German capital.

The great powers, Britain, France and Russia, grew increasingly apprehensive of German ambitions. The only country with closer relations on the continent was Austria, ruled for sixty years by Francis (Franz) Joseph I of the Habsburg dynasty. A symbol of longevity, he had ascended the throne in revolutionary 1848, the year that had shaken the entire continent. Not surprisingly, the aging gentleman grasped little of what was going on.

The switches that would direct history onto the tracks of two world wars were located in Berlin.

TWO WORLD WARS AND AFTER

The Great War

COUNTLESS VOLUMES have been written about the causes and consequences of the First World War. Many people had been expecting a decisive conflict before 1914, and the time seemed to be ripe.

The spark that set off the powder keg in the Balkans was the assassination of Austrian Archduke Francis (Franz) Ferdinand at Sarajevo in Bosnia, which had been annexed by Austria-Hungary, with German backing, in 1908. The Austrians believed that the group of young men who carried out the assassination had been hired and trained in neighboring Serbia, the main obstacle to further Austro-Hungarian expansion in the Balkans. Nevertheless, the elderly Emperor Francis Joseph was not immediately prepared to heed his advisers and declare war upon this small kingdom without Germany's agreement. In fact, Emperor William II had been waiting for just such an opportunity. The precarious balance of power among the European nations had shifted through the huge concentration of industrial and military might in the heart of the continent, in Germany. As every country mobilized, soldiers were sent off with flowers, and patriotic songs on their lips. Rulers dreamed up fine phrases. William, for example, declared: "There are no more political parties; I see only Germans."

The war and its aftermath have been chronicled in innumerable diaries, memoirs and novels; whole armies of historians have dissected and debated every aspect, from military strategy and the war economy to the ultimate collapse of Germany and Austria-Hungary. While no justification can be found for the senseless carnage in the trenches, one positive outcome of the war was the change it wrought in the status of workers, women and children in Germany, as in other belligerent states. However strange it may seem, the war exerted a democratic influence. In the army the rank and file was, of course, made up of industrial laborers, who learned how to handle and use guns. Women replaced their menfolk in industry, and this did more for their emancipation than any amount of feminist agitation. Children were left to themselves and had to go out to work at an even earlier age than before. The initial enthusiasm of eighteen-year-olds eager for action and their sudden sobering up in the trenches are vividly described in *All Quiet on the Western Front* by the German novelist Erich Maria Remarque.

The British naval blockade strangling the German economy induced the High Command to start indiscriminate submarine warfare. When the liner *Lusitania* was sunk, sending 1200 civilians to their death at the bottom of the ocean, Admiral Tirpitz ironically commented, "It is truly incredible to what extent we have become the most hated nation in the world." Who knows whether the United States might not have remained neutral if the Germans had not begun torpedoing its ships on the high seas.

Germany and Austria-Hungary found themselves up against the rest of the world, against everyone fit to bear arms or manufacture armaments. As a last resort, Russian revolutionary Vladimir Ilyich Ulyanov, better known as Lenin, was allowed to cross war-torn Germany in a sealed train. The Germans believed that his radical ideas would slow down the Russian war machine and bring Germany relief. They were right, in part, for Russia soon withdrew from the war, but the germ of revolution did not stop at the trenches and barbed wire. Peace was now demanded by German soldiers and sailors as well.

In October 1918 the German High Command under Field Marshal von Hindenburg and chief of staff Ludendorff realized that they would have to seek peace. The country was economically paralyzed; hunger and epidemics, depression and despair, had broken the will to continue.

The Weimar Republic

Events moved fast. On November 7 sailors in northern Germany seized power, on November 8 a republic was proclaimed in Munich, on November 9 the revolutionary spark spread to the capital, Berlin, on November 10 Kaiser Wilhelm fled to Holland. The abdication of the other German kings and princes followed, and their states became republics. The entire country was shaken by risings on both the right and the left. A united Germany was born on February 6, 1919, when a provisional constitution was proclaimed by the national assembly meeting in a Weimar theater where the tragedies of Goethe and Schiller had been performed for over a century — hence the names Weimar republic and Weimar constitution. A Social Democratic politician and former saddler, Friedrich Ebert, was elected the first president of the new republic.

Germany was now a federation of 17 'free lands' *(Länder)* – Prussia, Bavaria, Saxony, Württemberg, etc. Still a part of Germany were the free Hanseatic cities: Hamburg, Bremen and Lübeck. Beside the constitution there was also the peace treaty concluded at Versailles, where the Prussian king had been crowned German emperor in 1871. This demarcated new frontiers, leaving outside Germany a tenth of its population, admittedly only half of them speaking German as their mother tongue. But lost with these territories were many coal mines, ceded to France in the west, to Poland in the east. Moreover, the peace treaty imposed heavy war reparations, all the more difficult to pay as the country had been completely devastated. Nationalists invented the myth whereby Germany had not lost the war on the battlefield but through 'a stab in the back' from internal enemies.

The constitution had many weaknesses. It was not always clear what was under the jurisdiction of the individual German *Länder*, or the state as a whole. Germany was still called the *Reich* (empire); its president bore the title *Reichspräsident* – imperial president, as if the republic were merely provisional. He could dissolve parliament and call new elections, appoint the chancellor (prime minister), actually retaining many of the emperor's prerogatives. The successive governments were weak, and too many parties were represented in parliament. Frequent elections made it impossible to achieve any kind of stability.

War losses and heavy reparations triggered off the greatest inflation in the history of mankind, beginning in 1922 and culminating in 1923. In

94. The old part of Düsseldorf is a lively place with its many taverns and small breweries serving their own draft beer, its bars and cafés popular with the artistic crowd. The birthplace of the poet Heinrich Heine (in 1797), the city awards an annual prize bearing his name, for achievements in the cultural field. Düsseldorf's elegant shops also make it one of the most expensive cities in Germany.

95. Cologne (Köln) at night – a view of the old cathedral and the new museums: the Wallraf-Richarts Museum of modern art and the outstanding Roman-German Museum displaying archeological finds from the region. Cologne cathedral, a gem of German Gothic architecture, begun in 1248, is the largest church in Germany, and also has the world's largest hanging bell, St Peter's, weighing 25 tons. ▷

relation to the American dollar and 1914 rate of exchange, inflation reached 940 percent by July 1920, 427,900 percent by January 1923, and an unpronounceable 219,400,000,000,000 percent by November 1923. Money was carried in suitcases to buy a loaf of bread. But money is merely a piece of printed paper. As the mark deteriorated, the actual value of goods increased, exchanging hands in different ways, primarily through barter. The painful lesson learned in the early 1920s was passed on to future generations and reflected in the German attitude toward money and fear of inflation. Through inflation the rich became richer, and the poor destitute. In the general turmoil, political assassination was not uncommon. Right-wing anarchists murdered not only Communist politicians Rosa Luxemburg and Karl Liebnicht, flinging their corpses into the Landwehrkanal in Berlin, but also finance minister Erzenberger and foreign minister Rathenau. After the death of Friedrich Ebert in 1925, Marshal Paul von Hindenburg was elected president.

Hindenburg became leader of his country at the age of seventy-eight, never having espoused republican ideas. All the same, he worked for peace and order, as he understood them. Opposing him was his wartime subordinate and associate, General von Ludendorff, who had a prominent role in an abortive nationalist *coup d'état* in Munich in 1923. Here Ludendorff was assisted by an unknown agitator, ex-corporal Adolf Hitler.

Industry, which had profited during inflation, emerged from it in shambles. Realizing that Germany, even with the best intentions, could not pay the heavy reparations, the victors became more conciliatory. They could not take the chance of the region becoming too unstable politically, for in the east, instead of the Russian empire, the Soviet Union was pressing forward. Essential economic reforms were carried out and deflationary measures drafted. Germany once more achieved a certain degree of prosperity.

These favorable trends were interrupted by the worldwide economic depression. In early 1929 Germany reported two million unemployed; by 1932 the number had doubled. The generation that had experienced the rigors of inflation was again in a hopeless situation, condemned to idleness, awaiting some new figures on the political scene to come to their rescue. Sure enough, such figures appeared.

Political parties did not fight simply for votes but, with all means available, among themselves and in the streets, organizing small private armies for the purpose. The Communist and Social Democratic parties began to show firmer opposition to the rising National Socialist German Workers' Party. Its leader, Adolf Hitler, following the unsuccessful *Putsch* with Ludendorff when he was given a brief prison term, promised the workers employment and social security, and guaranteed the property of industrialists and landowners. While in prison, he wrote a book entitled *Mein Kampf* (My Struggle), in which he blamed the Jews for all ills and vowed to drive them from public life. Though the book was not taken very seriously, by 1928 its author had gained over 800,000 votes, and in 1930 six and a half million Germans voted for him.

Hindenburg had earlier declared that he would never speak with 'that Bohemian corporal', alluding to the fact that Hitler had been born in Austria and had taken out German citizenship only when he entered politics. Now, he had no choice but to receive him.

In the meanwhile, in the large German cities the arts were flourishing. Berlin had become a pulsating center of culture and entertainment, rivaling Paris. Personalities who had formed an intellectual opposition in

the time of the empire now came to the fore. Never before had there been so much bold, successful experimentation. Interested visitors, French and English, Russians and Japanese, came to see what was happening and left traces of their own original colors on this palette of diverse creativity. As a center of finance, trade and industry, Berlin boasted a public that was capable of appreciating and paying for all this. Historian Golo Mann puts it well: "One ought to speak of the Berlin, not of the Weimar republic."

The Birth of the Third Reich

As it turned out, the cultural life of the élite and the daily events of ordinary life bore little relationship to one another. The Weimar republic stumbled from one crisis into another. In the meantime President von Hindenburg celebrated his eighty-fifth birthday. Hitler became the leader of the strongest party at the parliamentary elections, and on January 30, 1933, Hindenburg had to appoint him chancellor and allow him to form a government. None of the commentators of the period thought that the man would stay in power. Most of the ministers in his cabinet were not from his party. Nevertheless, he managed to name his most loyal supporters to key posts. Thus, a First World War aviator decorated for bravery, Hermann Göring, became premier of Prussia and at the same time minister of the interior for the *Reich*. After a flying accident Göring had been treated with morphine for some time and was now addicted to the drug. This was the man who took control of all the police forces, including his most powerful tool, the secret police – *Geheime Staatspolizei*, better known by its abbreviated form as the Gestapo.

On February 27, a month after Hitler came to power, a fire broke out in Berlin's monumental parliament building, the *Reichstag*. Arrested on the spot was a Dutchman, Van der Lubbe, who had obviously started the blaze. Most historians, however, believe that the arson should be attributed to Hitler's organization and the Dutchman was simply a puppet in their hands. The Communists were promptly blamed and many, including members of parliament, were placed under arrest. The trial in Leipzig, at which Göring himself was a very inept witness, failed to prove that the Communists had been in any way involved. Yet fresh elections were immediately called. Hitler won only a relative majority of 44 percent, but in coalition with the small German National Party he commanded a majority of 18 deputies in parliament. Now he could form a government with only his own supporters and think about obtaining the two-thirds majority needed to change the constitution.

As the parliamentary building had to be renovated, the deputies met in the Kroll Opera House, formerly specializing in operettas. The Social Democratic opposition was simply barred from entry. A law was enacted, later called in German *Ermächtigungsgesetz* – Enabling Law, whereby the government could issue decrees independently of parliament for a period of four years. Hitler could now do what he liked without changing the constitution. Formally speaking, Hindenburg could have refused to sign the law, but he either no longer understood what was happening or actually approved of it.

Step by step, yet surprisingly quickly, the National Socialists carried out what they euphemistically called the process of *Gleichschaltung* – co-ordination. All powers in the state and every area of public activity, the judiciary and chambers of commerce, publishing and art associations, were soon firmly in their hands. By means of public works, highway

115. Johann Wolfgang Goethe (1749–1832), Germany's finest poet, was born in Frankfurt on Main and died in Weimar. In the duchy of Weimar he became a close adviser of Charles Augustus, to all intents and purposes his premier and principal minister in charge of several departments. Goethe's other interests were anatomy, physics and paintings, he managed the theater, translated and studied the history and literature of distant lands – in a word, a man of universal talents, like the principal character of his masterpiece, 'Faust'.

construction, for example, and investment in the armaments industry, unemployment was resolved. The Jews were excluded from public affairs. Concentration camps were built for political enemies, who were interned without a regular trial.

World War II

Flouting its international commitments, Germany regained the Saar in 1935, reoccupied the demilitarized Rhineland in 1936, and in 1938 first annexed Austria, then moved into the Sudetan region of Czechoslovakia. In March 1939 Hitler made the whole of Czechoslovakia a protectorate. All this was prepared and accompanied by an unprecedented propaganda campaign, while the western powers, France and Great Britain, looked on, taking no serious action. Italian dictator Mussolini became Hitler's closest ally, and distant Japan the third partner. Then, out of the blue, a pact was concluded with the Soviet Union, and Germany, now feeling safe to continue its conquests, invaded Poland on September 1, 1939. The western democracies finally reacted and the Second World War began.

In a year and a half the German war machine conquered all the non-neutral states of western and northern Europe, with the notable exception of Great Britain, taking one country after another in a 'lightning war', the *Blitzkrieg*. Encouraged by his successes, Hitler turned on the U.S.S.R. in June 1941, and before winter set in his armies stood before Moscow and Leningrad, then pushed on toward the Caucasus and swept across North Africa. He began to fulfill his evil promise, exterminating some six million European Jews, many in specially constructed gas chambers. The fortunes of war turned only when the United States entered the conflict, and the Soviets managed to organize the vast potential of their Asian expanses. Foot by foot in bloody battles, with resistance movements developing in many countries, the Germans were driven out of the regions they had occupied. Finally the victorious Allies found themselves in Germany itself.

Heavily bombed from the air, the German cities lay in ruins. Without any prospect of victory, German troops continued to defend themselves. On July 20, 1944, a group of officers, realizing the hopelessness of the situation, plotted to assassinate Hitler and thus terminate the senseless destruction. They failed. Regardless of impending defeat, the *Führer* was determined that Germany should fight on to the bitter end, whatever the consequences.

Hitler seems to have imagined some kind of cataclysmic collapse, a *Götterdämmerung*, as in German epic or Wagnerian opera, stating openly that the German people did not deserve to outlive him. Holed up in his Berlin bunker, he married his mistress of several years' standing, celebrating with champagne and waltz music, before committing suicide together with his wife. Propaganda minister Goebbels likewise killed himself, his wife and six children, as did later the infamous SS chief Himmler when he was arrested in the uniform of an ordinary sergeant. Because of Hitler's 'orgiastic dream of power' over four million German soldiers had died, and half a million civilians perished in bombing raids.

The act of unconditional surrender was signed by General Jodl on May 7, 1945. There was never a peace treaty, for there was no one to sign it. In the summer of 1945 most towns were in ruins, many able-bodied men were held in prisoner-of-war camps, while the majority of the population had no means of subsistence, nothing to do, no place to live. All authority was in the hands of military commanders, for the whole of Germany – including the capital Berlin – was divided into four occupation zones, American, British, French and Russian. In 1918, after the First World War, the emperor had fled, the monarchy was overthrown, but the state continued to exist, the administration functioned, remnants of the armed forces survived. In May 1945, however, there was no longer any German government, military or civilian.

Twenty of the highest-ranking leaders of the *Reich* stood trial before the International Military Court in Nuremberg. At one point *Reichsmarschall* Göring whispered to Admiral Dönitz, "If it weren't for that damned Auschwitz. It's all Himmler's doing. Without Auschwitz we could defend ourselves honorably. This way we have no chance whatsoever. Whenever anyone mentions us, they think of Auschwitz and Treblinka..." In this respect Göring was right, for in the memory of mankind the twelve years of National Socialist rule will always be associated with the horrors of concentration camps like Auschwitz, Buchenwald, Dachau and others. Thirteen war criminals were sentenced to death by hanging at Nuremberg and executed on October 16, 1946, except for Göring, who a few hours before his execution was scheduled had swallowed poison, slipped to him somehow in his prison cell. The other seven were given prison terms.

East and West

As war operations ended, a steady stream of refugees began to arrive. On the one hand, there were Germans expelled from Poland, Czechoslovakia, Hungary and the Balkans seeking refuge in western Germany; on the other, there were refugees fleeing west from the Russian occupation zone, joined in 1946 by German prisoners of war, gradually being released and heading for home.

Until 1948 Germany was administered by an Allied Control Council consisting of representatives of the United States, U.S.S.R, Great Britain and France. In mid-1948 the Soviets withdrew their representative, the first act in the division of Germany. The occupation zones in the west merged and in 1949 formed the Federal Republic of Germany; somewhat later the Soviet occupation zone became the Democratic Republic of Germany.

The creation of two German states also marked the beginning of the cold war, the descent of the 'iron curtain' — to use Winston Churchill's memorable phrase. Berlin was situated in the middle of the East German state, yet all the vital functions of the western sector of the city were linked with the Federal German Republic, though it was not formally a part of it.

The Federal German Republic — as its name indicates — was a federation composed of provinces *(Länder)* with a fair amount of autonomy, the boundaries between them determined by the military commanders. Some of the *Länder*, like Bavaria, or the free city-republics of Hamburg and Bremen, were based on historical tradition, but in most cases the boundaries were drawn fairly arbitrarily, depending sometimes on how far the respective army units had advanced during the final military operations of World War II. Nevertheless, owing to the rapid improvement of the standard of living, the 'German economic miracle', West Germans soon grew accustomed to the new names for their *Länder* such as Nordrhein-Westfalen or Baden-Württemberg. In the west the Allies did not repeat the errors committed after the First World War by allowing the population to sink into a state of despair and apathy. True, the war industry was dismantled under the rationale of preventing another war on German soil. An estimated 500 to 600 million dollars' worth of installations were carted off as reparations, the result being that West German industry ended up with more modern plants than the winning powers.

The Basic Law – the constitution – of the Fedral German Republic was drafted under auspicious circumstances. It was the work of progressive-minded German lawyers still appalled by the horrors of Nazi rule but well aware of the failings of the formally democratic Weimar republic that had opened the door to dictatorship. Moreover, the British Labour Party, now in power, took a benevolent view of the social welfare features of this new German constitution, and the United States, whose government had little knowledge of Europe and Germany, was represented mostly by German Jews who had made a timely escape from their former home and returned as high-ranking American officers or advisers. As a result, an important principle in the new social order of the Federal German

'The Four Horsemen of the Apocalypse' by Albrecht Dürer, woodcut, c. 1497.

Republic was that property carried obligations; it did not speak of a free market economy but only a social market economy — *Soziale Marktwirtschaft* — implying the solidarity of the successful with the less prosperous classes of society.

During this period the dismantling of industry was being pursued in the Soviet zone much more rigorously. A planned economy modeled on the U.S.S.R. was introduced in the newly-formed state. Germans in the eastern state joked, with their characteristic sense of humor, that their Democratic Republic was 'the most disciplined barracks in the socialist camp'. Despite certain achievements, social security, subsidized rents and food prices, and the outstanding successes of G.D.R. athletes at world and European championships and the Olympics, more and more East German citizens grew dissatisfied with the lack of freedom of expression and much lower living standard. Desiring to flee to the west, they came up against heavily guarded borders; Berlin was even divided by a high wall, topped with barbed wire.

The world soon became accustomed to the idea of two German states, with two national anthems, two flags. When both were admitted to the United Nations, the division seemed permanent. The West German constitution, however, stated at the beginning that a basic aim was the 'reunification' of Germany, though few believed that it could be achieved in the foreseeable future. The impression was that a united Germany had been an interlude between 1871 and 1945. During this brief period it had three different forms: an empire until 1918, the Weimar republic until 1933, and then the frightful Nazi regime, Hitler's New Order, which had proclaimed itself 'the thousand-year *Reich*' and lasted only twelve years.

Despite all obstacles many East Germans kept trying to escape to the west. No small number even lost their lives on the ruthlessly guarded border, but attempts continued, multiplying especially after Mikhail Gorbachev came to power in the Soviet Union and embarked on a process of liberalization that was cold-shouldered by the East German leaders. While a popular slogan had previously advised, "To learn from the Soviet Union is to learn from victories," now a high-ranking bureaucrat commented, "If a neighbor changes his wallpaper, it does not mean we have to do the same." During the summer of 1989 the stream of refugees, particularly through Hungary and Austria, suddenly swelled into a flood. In the fall of the same year the streets and squares of East German cities were packed with demonstrators, but the faltering regime did not dare to issue orders to fire into the crowds. In a bloodless revolution unprecedented in modern Europe, the people forced their leaders to open the borders and resign.

Germany will remain without a third of the territory belonging to the empire in 1914, without a fourth of what it had in 1937 when Hitler launched his campaigns of aggrandizement. The present generation of Germans has become reconciled to the situation, especially since for decades very few Germans have lived in the parts which now belong to Poland and the Soviet Union: most had abandoned their former homes toward the end of the war or shortly after.

With a population of 76 million, a huge economic potential, and its geographical position as the heartland of Europe, Germany is the most important factor on a continent which for two thousand years has been considered the center of world events and is now involved in a process of drawing closer together.

Soviet dictator Stalin seems to have been right when he said, on the eve of victory over Nazi Germany, "The Hitlers of history may come and go, but the German people will remain."

PAGAN GODS AND CHRISTIAN CUSTOMS

Myths and Legends

MOST OF OUR KNOWLEDGE of North European mythology comes from two great works of early medieval Icelandic literature, the *Eddas*, one in prose, the other in poetic form. There is plentiful evidence, however, that Scandinavian and German traditional beliefs and legends bore a very close similarity. According to ancient Germanic mythology, most of the deities belonged to a race of gods, the Aesir, dwelling in the citadel of Asgard. Among them were the supreme deity Odin, other well-known gods like Thor, Tyr and Balder, and the goddesses Frigg, Nanna and Sif. There was also another divine race called the Vanir, deities of wealth, fertility and peace. Chief in this group of immortals was the god of fertility Frey, while Frigg (Freya) appears here, too, their father being Njörd. The conflicts between the Aesir and the Vanir, their reconciliation by treaty, and their subsequent intermingling may reflect the relations between farming and warrior tribes.

Odin, also called Woden or Wotan, Frigg's husband, is the supreme German divinity, the god of battle, protector of heroes and father of the slain. His sacred animals are the raven and the wolf. Two ravens called Hugin and Munin would often alight on his shoulders to whisper in his ear what they had seen, flying among mortals. The name Odin, or Woden, is connected with the German word *Wut*, 'fury', though an older meaning is 'excitement'. Thus, Woden was also the god of ecstasy and all kinds of magic, even poetry. In exchange for wisdom he sacrificed an eye, so that in sagas and epics he appears as a one-eyed warrior carrying a spear and wearing a blue cloak and floppy-brimmed hat. In northern Europe and England the fourth day of the week, Wednesday, is named after him, Woden's day.

An important concept in ancient German mythology was the cataclysmic end of the world known as Ragnarok. This would be the final event, the ultimate destruction, the twilight of the gods. When the end of the world came, it was believed the demon Fenrir, appearing in the form of a wolf, would devour Odin. In the early Middle Ages, i.e. well into the Christian era, Odin was portrayed, accompanied by his ravens and a deer, in combat with some kind of monster.

Loki, a male deity, yet often appearing in the form of a mare, is the father of Fenrir, born of his love for the ogress Angrbod. Loki's sisters are the serpent Midgard, whose immense body covers the earth, and Hel, queen of the underworld. The chief opponent of the serpent Midgard is the god Thor, who tries in vain to drive her away from the cosmic sea. When the end of the world comes, Midgard and Thor will kill one another.

One day, beginning to mistrust the wolf Fenrir, the gods of the Aesir decided to bind him with an unbreakable chain called Gleipnir, pretending it was just a bit of fun. As a pledge of this, the god Tyr heroically thrust his hand into the jaws of the wolf, which promptly bit it off when it realized the trick. The god is always portrayed as one-handed.

According to legend, Loki, cunning and mischievous, sometimes sides with and helps Odin, but more often opposes him. Loki will destroy the god of beauty and light, Balder, Odin's son, by persuading Balder's blind brother Hoder to throw a dart of enchanted mistletoe at him, thus unintentionally killing him. This will mark the beginning of Ragnarok, the end of the world.

Frigg, a very sensual goddess, not at all faithful to her husband, Odin, is nevertheless patroness of marriage and motherhood. In southern Germany she was called Frija, while the Lombards (Langobardi) worshiped her as Freya, and regarded her as their special protectress. Her name, translatable as both 'wife' and 'mistress', was given by the Germanic peoples to the weekday dedicated to Venus in Latin.

Thor, in Old Saxon Thunar or Donar, etymologically related to *Donner* ('thunder'), is Odin's son and presides over the weather, storms and fertility. His chariot was drawn across the skies by two goats. In the *Poetic Edda* he is described as the strongest of the gods, defending all the others from the giants, and if necessary from men, with his hammer, Mjölnir. His blessing was required for marriage, and he protected livestock and crops. The oak, the ancient Germans' favorite tree, was dedicated to Thor, who also had his day: Thursday. His wife, Sif, had long golden hair, supposedly symbolic of ripening wheat fields, which was cut off by Loki.

Nanna, Balder's wife, died of sorrow after her husband was slain through Loki's malice. Her name was used as a poetic form of address for young women. Her son Forseti, seated in the brilliantly lit hall of Glitnir, would mete out justice to both gods and men.

Among his other responsibilities, Odin had command over the Valkyries, their name meaning 'choosers of the dead'. These were sturdy maidens who would ride over battlefields choosing the warriors fated to meet a heroic death and go to Valhalla — hall of slain heroes — a splendid palace within Asgard, citadel of the gods. Covered with shields instead of tiles, the roof was supported not by pillars but by spears. Here the Valkyries would bring their chosen heroes, who had fought for Odin, serve them drink and entertain them. Hanging before the west door was a crucified wolf with an eagle hovering above, which explains the carved images of these creatures found on the wooden doors of north German houses. Valhalla had 640 exits for the heroes selected by Odin. In the retelling of legends the name Asgard slowly fell into disuse, replaced by Valhalla as the home of the Germanic gods, not just slain heroes.

Roman historian Tacitus, writing about the Germans and their customs in the first century A. D., had very sketchy ideas about their gods, especially their complex relations. The Germans, he wrote, had accepted the Roman gods, even offering human sacrifices to Mercury, but only animals, 'in accordance with ordinary civilized custom', to Hercules and Mars. The Egyptian goddess Isis was also worshiped by the Suebi. ''The Germans do not think it in keeping with the divine majesty to confine gods within walls or to portray them in the likeness of any human countenance. Their holy places are woods and groves and they apply the names of deities to that hidden presence which is seen only by the eye of reverence.''

Tacitus also describes various ways in which the ancient Germans

116. Stained-glass window in the church of St Catherine in Oppenheim, a small town famous for its wineries. The largest building in the community, the red sandstone church stands on a rise at the outskirts of the town, dominating the entire region. Begun in 1234 it was not finished until the late 15th century. The surrounding region is called Rheinhessen, producer of the famous Rhine wines, mostly Riesling and Silvaner.

117. The central square of idyllic Oppenheim on the left bank of the Rhine, between Worms and Mainz. In the later 13th century it was a free imperial town, but was later outstripped by other cities in the vicinity. Destroyed in the war against the French in 1689, it had better luck in later wars. Here, too, are the ruins of the once important castle of Landskron. ▷

118. Frankfurt on Main. The town hall known as der Römer ('the Roman') occupies what were originally 11 separate houses. First the name applied only to the middle building, since it was located on Römerberg (Roman hill). In 1405 it was purchased by the city council, which then bought up the adjoining houses. On the upper floor of the central building is the Imperial Hall, where coronation banquets for German emperors were held. ▷▷

sought omens and divined the future. They set most store by divination by means of pure white horses specially kept for this purpose in sacred groves and never used for work. On the behavior and neighing of the horses when yoked to a sacred chariot they would base decisions on what to do, for they believed the creatures to be 'privy to the gods' counsels'.

While Tacitus gives us a fascinating first-hand account of the ancient Germans, the most reliable and comprehensive source of information about the Germanic gods and mythical heroes is the Icelandic *Edda*, already mentioned. The extent to which the much later *Edda* texts faithfully reflect pagan tradition is still a subject of much heated scholarly debate.

The *Nibelungenlied* (Song of the Nibelungs) – the most important German epic – can be traced to the *Edda* but also to historical tradition. In this epic romance the brave, handsome Prince Siegfried slays a dragon, returns a stolen treasure hoard to the Nibelungs, a strange race of dwarfs, and in return receives a cap rendering him invisible. Having bathed in the dragon's blood, he becomes invincible, except for a vulnerable spot under his shoulder blade where an oak leaf fell and the dragon's blood did not touch his skin. He woos Kriemhild, sister of the Burgundian king, Gunther, fights bravely on his side in a battle against the Saxons, and promises to help him win Queen Brunhild, who is stronger and binds her suitor, hanging him on a nail. Siegfried, invisible, accompanies Gunther next time and conquers Brunhild on Gunther's behalf. As a reward he gets Kriemhild as his bride. The evil courtier Hagen manages to extract Siegfried's secret from Kriemhild, and kills him. Kriemhild then marries the Hunnish king, Etzel, (an allusion to the historical Attila) with the aim of one day avenging herself on the Burgundians for Siegfried's death. The opportunity eventually presents itself, and all the Burgundian royal party visiting Etzel's court are slain. Kriemhild kills the captured Hagen and is herself executed, the tale ending, as among the gods of the *Edda*, in general mayhem.

Influencing German folklore, the *Nibelungenlied* also served as a rich source of inspiration for German composers and poets of the nineteenth century. The *Edda* and *Nibelungenlied* are skilfully interwoven in Wagner's operatic tetralogy *Ring of the Nibelungs*.

To understand a nation and its country, it is important to know how it feels about its myths and, hence, how mythology will affect its actions. The nineteenth century took a romantic view of the old German sagas and the 'Song of the Nibelungs'. In the twentieth century, however, this tradition began to be compared with Christian civilization, and nationalists claimed its superiority over 'decadent' earlier beliefs. Characteristically, during the 1930s many Germans gave their children names from old German legends, suddenly producing a lot of little Siegfrieds, Balders and Brunhilds. Hitler not only enjoyed Wagner but even allowed what was for the great composer merely a fairy-tale to influence his political views. Toward the end of the Second World War, he believed he should bring about a final cataclysm, rather like the Twilight of the Gods, in which the flames devouring him and his henchmen would destroy all of Germany and, if possible, the whole continent.

In present-day Germany ancient Germanic mythology is little known. The time has also passed when progressive-minded people avoided Wagner's works, considering them 'fascist', though Wagner, who died in 1883, truly cannot be blamed for the fact that Adolf Hitler had a passion for his operas, for which the composer wrote both the libretto and the score.

136

119. Dinkelsbühl, a district seat in northern Bavaria, is located in a valley on the old road from Augsburg to Würzburg, the Romantic Road as it is called, because of the many picturesque spots it passes through. This well-preserved medieval town, noted for its attractive half-timbered houses, now has a population of only 10,000. In the 15th-century castle, a children's festival (Kinderzeche) is held every year in memory of the Swedish occupation of 1632, during the Thirty Years' War.

120. The park in Oppenheim (Rhineland Palatinate).

121. Thatch roofing is an attractive feature of many rural dwellings, though more common in the north of the country. In parts with heavy snowfalls it is less practical, though a good insulator.

122–124. In the 14th century the princes of Schaumburg built a moated castle at Bückeburg, around which a town gradually developed. The Schloss was rebuilt in Renaissance style in the 16th century with four wings around a rectangular courtyard, and subsequently given many Baroque features, such as its ornate gateway and opulent 'golden' salon. Now a museum, it houses a large art collection.

123

125. Carnivals and festivals of all kinds are a traditional feature of German life, giving an opportunity to forget about work and let one's hair down. These two girls were pictured enjoying the annual wine festival in Nuremberg.▷

126. Germany would not be a land of musicians if one counted only its greatest composers like Bach or Beethoven. Even the smallest town has its own amateur brass band, which makes up for any lack of skill with sheer enthusiasm, playing on every possible occasion, at various ceremonies and festivals.

127. A fondness for dressing up in historical costumes and fanciful attire seems to be a national characteristic. Here the excuse is a ceremony during the Nuremberg wine festival. This city has good reason to be proud of its medieval past. Living here at the same time were artist Albrecht Dürer (1471–1528), poet and Meistersinger Hans Sachs (1494–1576), the inventor of the pocket watch, Peter Henlein (1480–1542), and of the first globe, Adam Kraft (1455–1508). All of them probably enjoyed the ancient vintage festivities in their day.

128

128. The Schloss of Ludwigsburg (Baden-Württemberg) is a popular place to get married. In an attempt to imitate court life at Versailles, Duke Eberhard Ludwig built this great complex of 18 buildings with over 400 rooms in the first half of the 18th century. A stylish wedding in the ducal palace is followed by a photo session in the courtyard — one wonders only how the bride's train will fit into the tiny sports car.

129

129. The smile beneath the raised bridal veil seems to confirm that marriage has a future even in this day and age. Though young Germans prefer casual clothing for everyday wear, most choose traditional formal dress for weddings, adding if possible great-grandmother's veil, tucked away in an old chest for the great day.

130. A young bridal couple after their wedding breakfast in front of the Gasthaus zur Linde in Memmingen. The population of Germany is declining. In spite of the country's prosperity, more and more marriages are childless or with only one child.

131

131, 132. *Osnabrück cathedral: the elaborately worked doorway enclosing the choir ambulatory, and a medieval reliquary in the rich treasury. Dedicated to St Peter, the cathedral (Dom) was begun in the 11th century but not completed until the 16th — hence its mixture of Romanesque and Gothic styles. For long a center for trade between the Rhineland and Baltic coast, Osnabrück reached the peak of its prosperity in the 18th century.*

153

133

133. The old coat of arms of the city of Ravensburg (Baden-Württemberg). The gabled town hall was built in the second part of the 14th century; parts of its façade, particularly the portico, are fine examples of Renaissance architecture.

134. Tapestry in the splendid Baroque Schloss of Bruchsal, built between 1720 and 1760 by a local prince bishop. It is famous for the remarkable staircase designed by architect Balthasar Neumann, and for its annual concerts. Destroyed during the war, the whole vast complex has now been completely reconstructed.

136

137

135. A decorative ornament on a façade in Biberach (Baden-Württemberg), a medieval town on the banks of the Riss. These signs are found not only on inns, but on the houses of merchants and craftsmen, sometimes simply because prosperous middle-class families wanted emblems similar to the heraldic insignia of the German aristocracy.

136. A bourgeois coat of arms on a house in Dettelbach. The town is known for its extensive medieval walls with 53 towers and five gates, surrounded by a deep moat. The 17th-century pilgrimage church of Maria im Sand (Our Lady of the Sands) has a huge Rococo altar and an organ dated 1659 built by Peter Scholl and still in use.

137. Ornaments on a façade and rooftop in the small town of Bruchsal. Best known for its huge Schloss, it has an attractive public park with a Baroque belvedere. From the large church of St Peter, built in the mid-18th century by architect Balthasar Neumann, one can see as far as the Rhine valley and the Pfälzer Wald forest.

138. *Young Germans know they won't have much of a career without an education. The demanding high-school curriculum gives them a heavy reading load. Today fewer girls aspire to the traditional role of* Hausfrau. *The feminist movement is active and not a single political party dares to disregard issues relating to women.*

140. Hameln (in English Hamelin) is familiar because of the legend of the Pied Piper who delivered the town from a plague of rats. As the piper played, the rats followed him, charmed into an abyss. When the town council refused to pay the agreed sum, he played his pipe again and this time all the children followed him, never to return. The costumed piper in the picture merely wants to charm a few marks from the pockets of passers-by.

141. Daring displays of skateboard virtuosity are not uncommon, and this picture would scarcely deserve attention if it had not been taken in Leipzig, in what was formerly East Germany.

139. Street entertainers are a famialiar sight in many German towns, which in recent years have become much more lively and colorful.

142. Though Boppard on the Rhine is in a famous wine-producing region, marksmen here seem to prefer beer. Sharpshooting societies with their uniforms and medals, awarded every year at contests, were founded in the Middle Ages by artisans and tradesmen, who wanted the same privilege of handling arms as the aristocracy.

141

143–147. Typical examples of windows and doors in Saarbrücken, capital of one of Germany's smallest units, Saarland, on the Franco-German border. Its proximity to France is reflected in its urban architecture, and even more in the tasty local cuisine. In the 18th century, Prince William Henry of Nassau-Saarbrücken enlarged the town, raising some fine Baroque buildings. The Schloss built in the same period was burned down in 1793 during the French Revolution, but later reconstructed.

148

148. A terracotta theater mask in the Roman-German Museum in Cologne (Köln). As Colonia Agrippina, Cologne was an important Roman settlement from the 1st century A.D. The large and well-designed archeological museum, opened in 1974, has assembled finds unearthed in this region, giving an excellent picture of life here in Roman times.

149. A strikingly realistic Pietà from the late 14th century in the Franciscan church in Coblenz. Strategically located at the confluence of the Rhine and Mosel, on the site of a Roman camp, the city has several fine Romanesque and Gothic churches with outstanding works of medieval art.

150. A landscape near Landshut in Lower Bavaria. Back in Roman times, Tacitus already noted that Germany had 'a good soil for growing cereal crops'. ▷

151. In the town of Rothenburg on the Tauber, a performance entitled 'Drink' (Der Trunk) is given every year on All Souls Day in memory of a siege laid by Count Johannes Tilly in 1631, during the Thirty Years' War. The town has preserved its traditions, and young people like to dress up in the old costumes.

152. A landscape near Bamberg. All over the western part of Germany, modern highways have swallowed up sizable chunks of farmland and forest.

153. Poppies amid fields of wheat. Germany is self-sufficient in some food production, but in general its agriculture lags behind industry in terms of efficiency.

The old German customs still in evidence have no connection with ancient Germanic mythology: for the most part they date from the early period of Christianity in these parts.

The carnival, celebrated during the days preceding Lent, came to Germany from the south. The name is associated by popular etymology with *carne vale,* Italian for 'Flesh, farewell'. Regardless of its Christian associations, the custom can definitely be traced back to the Roman Saturnalia, which may explain why the center of the carnival celebrations in Germany is in Cologne and Mainz, cities with an ancient Roman tradition. The first written record of the Cologne carnival dates back to 1341. In other parts of Germany the custom is called *Fastnacht* (*fasten* = to fast, *nacht* = night), and in Bavaria and Austria *Fasching,* derived from the same root.

Like the Romans, the old Germans celebrated the coming of Spring with feasting, carousing, and a general release of sensual passion. In the days before the Lenten period of fasting and abstinence, Christian morality was somewhat relaxed. The carnival likewise gave the common people a brief respite from the rigid class system, for social distinctions were concealed by fanciful masks and costumes. In feudal times it was a moment of democracy when everybody could mingle and enjoy themselves despite barriers of property and birth. Citizens took the opportunity to organize jousts and tournaments, otherwise the privilege of the aristocracy. Though the carnival today no longer has the same egalitarian function, people of all social levels enjoy dressing up and wearing humorous or hideous masks.

While a medieval carnival was truly an unbridled, licentious affair, the appearance of the venereal disease, syphilis, brought to Europe by sailors, caused a sudden change in sexual behavior. Seen as the 'scourge of God', the disease was generally regarded as divine punishment for immorality. Thus, the most debauched of the carnival customs were suppressed, more through fear of incurable disease than from dread of Judgment Day. However, satirical songs, feasting, drinking and dancing remained popular. Folk art found a creative outlet in the old masks, made of leather, fabrics and deftly woven straw, which were often more original than today's concoctions of rubber and plastic. In earlier times people liked to dress up as devils or witches, knights or ladies-in-waiting, or even priests – a way of poking fun at them. Apart from covering their faces, women would reveal as many of their charms as possible. These days the masks often caricature well-known politicians or other figures in the public eye.

Carnival revels are understandably typical of the part of Germany where Roman Catholics predominate. Protestants, always opposed to any form of 'perversion', extravagant display or unseemly behavior, were too strict and serious-minded for masked processions, too puritanical to permit themselves such liberties, albeit only once a year. Even today the carnival is not celebrated in northern Germany with its Protestant majority.

The revelry ends on the first Wednesday of the forty-day Lenten period before Easter – in German called *Aschermittwoch* (Ash Wednesday). In the Rhineland, another venerable name for this is *Wiwerfastelobend* (widows' carnival night), when the womenfolk, even widows, could do as they pleased. In many German cities it is the custom on this day for a secretary to cut off her boss's necktie, the symbolism here being quite explicit. After this the women are free to leave their workplace and celebrate as they like.

154. Young Germans differ little in tastes and habits from their counterparts in other economically advanced countries. Less radical in their political views than they were in the 60s, they are more concerned these days with environmental issues.

The Passion Play

Another German custom, as old as the carnival and also connected with Christian tradition, but much more serious and ambitious, is the performance of miracle plays depicting the Passion of Christ *(Passionspiele)*. These dramatizations of the sufferings and death of Jesus Christ are performed entirely by amateurs – prominent citizens or simple farmers. Even before they appeared in the thirteenth and fourteenth centuries, virtually in the same form as today, there were older Easter plays *(Osterspiele)*. Later expanded, the Passion plays treat not only the events preceding Easter and the Resurrection but the whole of Christian teaching on salvation. From the fourteenth century on they were organized in many places, lasting for several days with thousands of participants. These plays were not approved by the Protestants, so wherever Protestantism gained the upper hand, such performances ceased. Luther's followers felt that Christ's Passion was far too solemn and sacred a matter for play acting.

The most celebrated dramatization of the Passion, organized almost without interruption since 1633, takes place in Oberammergau, a village in the district of Garmisch-Partenkirchen in the Bavarian Alps. This idyllic spot near the source of the Ammer River at an altitude of 2800 feet is a well-known summer and winter resort, noted for its wood carvers. Oberammergau's biggest drawing card, though, is its renowned Passion play, performed in recent times every four years.

The play originated in a vow made by the villagers after a terrible epidemic of the Black Death in 1633. The grateful survivors pledged to re-enact the drama of Christ's final days on earth every ten years. In return they expected the Almighty to protect the village in the future, and as far as is known, the plague never reappeared in these parts.

Chivalric Societies

Another tradition of long standing in Germany is embodied in the local shooting societies *(Schützengesellschaft)*, actually a relic from medieval times when craft guilds were thriving in the towns and prosperous artisans tried in various ways to emulate the aristocracy and knightly orders. Their festivals became the equivalent of chivalric tournaments. On the day of the annual shooting festival, usually in early May when the weather was suitable, big contests were organized. In those times hunting was a strictly guarded privilege of the aristocracy, and commoners could shoot only as a pastime – the term 'sport' was not yet in use – or take the risk of poaching, for which penalties were severe.

The first contests were in shooting down a bird in flight, later superseded by target shooting. Successful competitors received decorative medals, while the top marksman every year was named *Schützenkönig* ('King of the Sharpshooters'). In many places in Germany, especially in the south, the custom has been preserved and the *Schützenkönig* is still a local celebrity. In 1989 the Federal Republic of Germany had 12,000 registered clubs for this sport.

Sentimental about their medieval period, Germans enjoy dressing up as personages of that age. In present-day Germany the cult of knightly orders is still cherished, and there are people who will spend lavishly to appear once a year in old costumes and uniforms, resplendent with large feather hats and drawn swords, parading in front of their friends.

The most important of these organizations, the Teutonic Order *(Der deutsche Orden)*, or Teutonic Knights of St Mary's Hospital at Jerusalem, was founded at Acre in Palestine in 1190, during one of the Crusades. After 1837 it was reorganized and established in nearly all the German provinces, enjoying the support of German sovereigns. The medal for bravery in combat, the Iron Cross, first awarded in the Prussian army in the early nineteenth century, was in fact inspired by the cross worn by members of the Teutonic Order. The order's one-time wealth can be judged by the number of estates and castles it possessed. Its present headquarters, in Austria, is right next to St. Stephen's Cathedral in the very heart of Vienna, where it has stood for centuries. It also owned the castle of Brühl near Bonn, used by the West German government for its most elegant receptions. As the twentieth century draws to a close, the Teutonic Order has no special social function, but among the middle class, university professors, lawyers, and industrialists, conservatives who would like, if only occasionally, to dress up as knights, it still finds new acolytes.

A less respectful attitude towards knightly organizations is found in the Order of Jesters (Schlaraffien). Schlaraffenland in German means Land of Cockaigne, where it is forbidden to work and where roast pigeons fly right into people's mouths. The Order of Jesters was founded in 1859 as a society for 'cultivating sociability, art and humor'. After taking examinations in different branches of art, its members were promoted from apprentice to journeyman, master, and finally 'knight'. Wearing blue and yellow silk jester's caps with bells, they engaged in 'duels', which consisted of composing mocking poems about one another, and reciting or singing them in front of the society. The society judged the winners, who received mock medals that they would attach to their caps, and when the caps were covered, blue and yellow scarfs. Even today a member can count on hospitality from others of his order when visiting places where the society has branches.

A much more significant role in German public and business life was played by student corporations known as the Burschenschaft. These, too, were in a sense inspired by knightly orders, even teaching their members the use of arms. They also wore caps and scarfs in special colors, but it was all taken very seriously. If something is taken too seriously, Germans say bierernst, meaning 'earnest as beer'. The expression probably comes from the student corporations: at their meetings members were supposed to prove their virility by drinking large quantities of the beverage with great solemnity. There are two typical images of the student corporations: drinking beer in a specially reserved room at an inn, and fighting duels.

Up to 1918 the ceremonial opening of the Parliament took place in Berlin castle.

171

Student duels called *Mensur* were fought over the slightest, even imaginary, offence. The weapons used were sabers specially designed for slashing rather than thrusting, since the purpose of the duel was not to kill, but to inflict a visible injury, if possible on the opponent's face. A scar received in a student duel was called a *Schmiss*. In Germany during the second half of the nineteenth and first half of the twentieth century, these ugly scars indicated that the bearer had been a member of a student corporation and fought a duel. In certain circles they were deemed a mark of distinction, proof that the bearer had studied at a good German university, and was politically a conservative nationalist. Many corporation members were to be found in the legal profession and among high-ranking civil servants.

When students graduated, they generally remained members of their corporations as *alte Herren* ('old gentlemen'), regularly attending beer-drinking sessions. Here they met young corporation members, who could later count on their wholehearted assistance when entering professional life. Membership of an influential corporation was generally a guarantee of a post in the state administration, judiciary or some other important field. After the Second World War their influence waned; facial scars ceased to be regarded as a mark of distinction, though they are still seen. According to figures for the early 80s, in West Germany there were 116 corporations at 31 universities, though with only a few thousand members, and over 20,000 *alte Herren*.

Oktoberfest

One festival inspired by venerable customs that attracts great crowds from Germany and abroad is the *Oktoberfest* in the Bavarian capital of Munich. For most visitors, attending the *Oktoberfest* means going to a large field in the city where pitched tents and kiosks offer Bavarian specialties, and beer flows in vast quantities. Like a huge fair, the festival includes a host of other attractions. The locals wear their traditional attire, the men in hunting jackets and the girls and women in dirndl skirts. It is interesting that Bavarians consider their folk costume formal dress. Conservative Bavarian politicians or businessmen will turn up wearing a hunting jacket at a reception where others are in dinner jacket or tails, the ladies in long evening gowns. This attire is also a political statement. At elections, the bushy-mustached, green-jacketed gentleman driving the latest BMW will cast his vote for the right-wing Bavarian national party (CSU), long led by the late Franz Josef Strauss. Even Social Democrats, if they have any ambitions in this city, cannot avoid some of the festivities, for example, the ceremonial opening, at which the mayor taps the first barrel of beer, preferably with one blow and spilling as little liquid as possible – a skill that requires much practice.

The *Oktoberfest*, which now lasts for sixteen days, was first celebrated on October 13 and 14, 1810, when King Maximilian I Joseph staged festivities in honor of his son's marriage. In 1985 there was some discussion as to whether to celebrate the 150th or 175th anniversary, since the festival had been canceled 25 times in the past 175 years. In any case, it was a record-breaking occasion – seven million visitors, who drank 10 million pints of beer and consumed, among other edibles, 660,000 roast chickens. The *Oktoberfest* has become, in its way, a symbol of the modern Germany, which shows no interest in armaments, which is not gloomy and humorless, nor isolationist, but wide open to the world, while still cherishing its distinctive features.

THE ECONOMIC MIRACLE

CERTAIN PREJUDICES exist about every nation. As German satirist Kurt Tucholsky (1890–1935) once wrote, "The English are the Romans of the new age. The French are the Chinese of the Occident. The Japanese are the the English of the Orient. But what sort of tribe the Bavarians might be, no one has figured out." According to the popular image, the typical German appreciates order, has a gift for organization, invention and enterprise, is willing to save and invest, and above all regards work not just as a means to earn a living but as the fundamental purpose of life. It is a widespread belief that nowhere else in the world – or at least in Europe – are diligence, perseverence and industry so deeply ingrained in the national character.

To understand Germany's economic rise in the twentieth century, it is better to forget national generalizations and begin with concrete facts. At the beginning of the century the national economies of Europe's industrialized countries were developing along similar lines. Differences were determined by natural wealth, primarily mineral resources, agricultural possibilities and population density. The First World War was waged *inter alia* – and some believe primarily – to secure markets and a place in the sun. Germany paid a high price for defeat, losing 13 percent of its territory, 10 percent of its population, 15 percent of its arable land and 75 percent of its iron deposits; its capacities for crude iron production were reduced 44 percent, steel 38 percent, and coal 26 percent. Germany was thus obliged to import food and many raw materials. An equally onerous burden was the reparations to be paid to the victor nations. In 1921, after protracted negotiations, these were set at 132 billion marks – the equivalent of 31.5 billion dollars. Of this sum, France was to receive 52 percent, Great Britain 22 percent, Italy 10 percent, Belgium eight percent, the remainder to be shared by the other Allies.

With the cessation of hostilities, German families were naturally spared further anxiety about husbands, fiancés, brothers and sons fighting at the front, but psychologically, the postwar situation may have been even harder to bear. As long as the war lasted, there was always the hope that when it ended, everything would improve. Now, however, the disastrous inflation and then unemployment resulted in general discontent and depression. People worked more and had less, apart from a privileged, fortunate, or shrewd minority. There was a growing desire for revenge on wartime opponents, and mounting hatred and envy of those who had prospered.

In this period may lie some of the roots of the anti-Semitism that ended in what many consider the greatest crime in German history – the massacre of Jews during the Second World War. Until the 1920s anti-

The Price of Defeat

Semitism was no more rife here than in other western countries. The pogroms occurring in Poland and Russia were unknown in Germany. During the First World War many German Jews had displayed outstanding patriotism, received medals for bravery, distinguished themselves in the officer corps. After the full civil emancipation of the Jews in Germany in 1869, there were clear tendencies toward assimilation. According to the census of 1925, only 0.9 percent of the German population declared themselves as Jewish. True, a steady stream of Jews poured into Germany from the east – from Poland, the Ukraine and Russia. In their new country they were regarded as foreigners because of their dialect, manner of dress and Orthodox customs. They felt, however, that they had come to the 'homeland of their language', in the words of Ben Gorion, a writer from the Ukraine. Many of the Jews of eastern Europe communicated in Yiddish, which was based on the old language of central Germany with the addition of many Hebrew and Slavonic words.

Although the Jews were well represented in the professional classes, particularly among physicians, lawyers, pharmacists, what ordinary Germans noticed most was the Jewish tradesman. It was he who raised prices, and in inflationary times sold basic necessities on credit, charging 'usurious interest'. Big business, industry, mines, large banks and insurance companies were not owned by Jews, but the 'little man' had no contact with representatives of these higher spheres of the economy. The shopkeeper or small-time banker who was unpleasant to him was often a Jew.

Hitler's Solution

Hitler's propaganda claimed that power in the Weimar republic was in the hands of the Jews. Yet in 19 successive governments with 387 ministers, only two ministers (Preuss and Rathenau) were Jewish, i.e. 0.51 percent, less than the percentage of Jews in the total population. True, among the 44 Nobel-prize winners from Germany and Austria were 10 Jews and four of mixed Jewish descent, which amounts to 29.5 percent – far more than their share in the total population.

Probably one of the reasons for the success of Hitler's propaganda was its skillful combination of hatred of the rich – 'plutocrats' as he called them – with hostility to the Jews. Thus he adroitly won over Social Democratic and Communist supporters and steered popular resentment away from the German industrialists and bankers, who were naturally grateful.

But what use to the average German was his devotion to work if in 1928 seven percent, and in 1932, 30 percent of the employable had no jobs? This fact alone is sufficient to explain, economically and sociologically, the upheavals that were imminent.

When Hitler's National Socialist Party came to power, its speechmakers immediately began to distinguish between *das schaffende Kapital* ('creative capital') and *das raffende Kapital* ('greedy capital'). The latter, of course, was Jewish, or possibly belonging to other wealthy people who did not approve of the new regime. After that is was comparatively easy to launch slogans like *Gemeinnutz geht vor Eigennutz* (General welfare is more important than personal welfare – egoism).

The fact remains, however, that Hitler ended unemployment very quickly. A major factor here was the inauguration of an extensive program of public works: land improvement, flood control, and especially highway construction, as this had a certain military aspect. Under Hitler, industry received more and more orders from the army for armaments and military equipment, all financed by bonds.

Unemployment was also reduced by introducing the draft and, before this, militaristic work drives. In this way many unemployed youths were simply removed from the scene. A fair number found jobs in the newly-formed Nazi party bureaucracy, in the party's paramilitary SS and SA formations, and in the police. All this was based on rather dubious financing, more or less on credit, as economists realized, but not the man in the street. In the mid-30s Hitler and the people around him anticipated war, and calculated that the cost of Germany's new prosperity would be paid by those defeated on the battlefield. By 1936 full employment had been achieved, and real income, compared to 1932, had risen 21 percent. After these successes, any hopes that may have been entertained of containing the Nazis were shattered. They could do whatever they pleased. In every firm they had trusted agents called *Betriebsführer* ('company leader') who, at least theoretically, could even dismiss the directors.

The Wartime Economy

In the early 30s economics experts, especially in western countries, claimed that a 'war economy in peacetime' had been created in Germany, and that only war could secure additional raw materials, food staples, and even manpower, thereby averting the collapse of the economy, which German laborers believed was prospering. Hitler and his staff obviously knew this, too. The economic situation forced him to go to war before the country was militarily prepared for it. At the beginning of 1939 Germany still had to import 65 percent of its requirements in iron ore and petroleum, 80 percent of the textiles it needed.

Karl Hardach, a contemporary German economist, has divided Germany's wartime economy into three phases: the first was the *Blitzkrieg* ('lightning war') from the fall of 1939 until winter 1941/42, the second was the phase of 'increased economic effort' until the summer of 1944, and the third the remaining ten months of 'all-out effort'.

The first phase resembled peacetime production, even bringing the Germans some relief. Fast-moving armored divisions overran vast expanses of territory – Poland, France, Belgium, the Netherlands, Denmark, Norway, Yugoslavia and Greece – without too many casualties, and from that moment the potential of the occupied countries could be drawn upon. Germany was now well supplied with goods, even better than before the war, which had a positive psychological effect on the population, not yet exposed to widespread bombing of cities. But the tide of German successes – the victories of the summer of 1941, the thrust across the Ukraine and Russia, the seizure of extensive agricultural land, with the prospect of soon occupying the Caucasus oil fields – was abruptly turned by the onset of the dreaded Russian winter and Hitler's first major setbacks.

In January 1942 a leading journal, *Der deutsche Volkswirt* (German Economist), wrote: "The winter campaign has opened our eyes to the fact that the greatest military and economic efforts must be demanded of the German people." Between May 1939 and May 1941 the strength of the German armed forces was increased from 1.4 to 7.2 million, creating a manpower shortage. The problem was solved by recruiting foreigners, in most cases prisoners; in 1944 there were over seven million. The number of employed German women did not grow significantly, for soldiers' wives received adequate compensation, and when the bombing began, they were reluctant to leave their homes and children. A large portion of the labor force was naturally re-directed to activities directly related to the war effort. The increasing frequency of air raids also affected the economy; their aim was to slow down war production, interrupt communications, and generally demoralize the population, both civilians in the cities and soldiers at the front, anxious about the safety of their families at home. Nevertheless, war production accelerated: if figures for the first quarter of 1942 are indexed at 100, by the third quarter of 1944 the scale had reached a peak of 279, thanks in great part to the organizational ability of the new minister of armaments, architect Albert Speer.

After the war Speer said that Germany would have lost even if it had not been defeated on the battlefield, as it had run out of iron, petroleum and munitions. By the end of 1943, many generals and economists saw defeat as inevitable and recommended terminating the war, but Hitler viewed such advice as high treason. Propaganda chief Goebbels declared that if the Nazis lost the war, they would '...leave the stage, loudly slamming the door behind them!'

As the Allied forces closed in, Hitler ordered the destruction of all postal and power installations, railways, canals, even warehouses with whatever supplies remained. He believed that the German people did not deserve to survive, for they had lost the war. Speer and other more clear-headed Germans managed to scuttle this insane final decision, which they called 'Nero's orders'.

When military operations ended in May 1945, the victorious Allies nevertheless found a ravaged land. Railway transport was paralyzed, the tracks torn up, and over half the locomotives wrecked. Seventy percent of the bridges had been demolished, falling into rivers and canals and blocking the waterways, along with 1700 sunken ships. A quarter of all housing, in many cities two-thirds, and in Berlin three-quarters, had been destroyed. That this defeated, devastated country should have arisen again so quickly has been aptly called the 'German economic miracle'.

The Federal Phoenix

After the outbreak of the cold war, in particular, the United States and Great Britain aided the swift economic recovery of their zones. In this respect they had excellent German collaborators who, having learned from past misfortunes, in some ways surpassed their mentors. What was established in Germany was not simply a free market economy but, as always emphasized since the late 40s, a *social* market economy.

Much of the credit for the German economic miracle must go to Ludwig Erhard, first minister of economic affairs of the Federal Republic. In early 1948 he pointed out, "No one should doubt that I wish to create a situation in the economy that will ensure prosperity for broader sections of our people. From the outset it has been my desire, through a wide dispersion of massive purchasing power, finally to overcome the old conservative social structure!" And these words came from a right-wing politician, not a Social Democrat. Erhard, who could certainly be described as a liberal economist, belonged to the Christian Democratic Union (CDU), the furthest to the right of the major West German parties. At that time the CDU did not differ from the Social Democrats, many now returning from abroad or from concentration camps, in its determination

157.   A street scene in Bremen, Germany's smallest Land. Bremen with its port Bremerhaven has a very long tradition of independence, becoming a free Hanseatic city as early as the 14th century. Accounted the second oldest republic in Europe, it was first mentioned in chronicles in 787 as a Christian mission post for northern Europe.

158.   Old urban architecture is probably nowhere as beautifully preserved as in Bremen, where the merger of traditional and modern has been particularly successful. Developed mostly during the 15th century,

159

the city has many Gothic buildings, including the Rathaus with a huge wine cellar filled with enormous painted barrels.

159.   Bremen has commemorated in sculpture its own folk-tale, 'The Musicians of Bremen'. This is the story of a donkey, dog, cat and rooster who were not satisfied with their station in life and set out into the world. Beset by robbers, they barely escaped with their lives. The tale dates from the 12th century, when social classes were well defined and everyone knew his place in society. The sculptor is Gerhard Marcks.

160

160, 161. *Schloss Gottorf, picturesquely sited on a bend in the Schlei River on the outskirts of the charming town of Schleswig. The castle, built in the 12th century for the local bishop, was mostly reconstructed in the late 17th and early 18th in Baroque style as the residence of Danish kings. Gottorf, the largest Schloss in Schleswig-Holstein, now houses the state museum.*

162. The sea does not treat Schleswig-Holstein gently; wind and waves constantly erode the flat sandy coast. Much of it would be washed away if man did not protect it in various ways: by embankments, piles sunk in the water, even the propagation of certain kinds of crab and marine creatures.

162

164

163. A view of the canal leading from the Alster lake to the Elbe and of Hamburg town hall (late 19th century). Hamburg has two large lakes, the Outer and Inner Alster, actually widenings in the Alster River, a tributary of the Elbe, and a ramified canal system.

164. The fine buildings around the Inner Alster were reconstructed after wartime bombing, when most of the inner city burned down. Along the waterfront and in side streets are the most fashionable shops and expensive

165

hotels. Nearby is the famous opera, one of the oldest in Germany, now in splendid new premises.

165. A statue on Hamburg's Rathausmarkt Square in front of the town hall. Germany's second largest city, Hamburg constitutes a separate Land. Founded in the 9th century, the town had achieved a high degree of independence by the 13th, when, together with Lübeck, it developed the Hanseatic League.

166

166. An arcade with cafés and elegant shops beside a canal in the center of Hamburg. Thanks to its overseas connections, Hamburg offers first-class goods from all over the world. The canals, like the one in the picture, are well maintained and navigable.

167

167, 168. Unlike preceding generations, German children are growing up without complexes or prejudices. Almost every school has a fair number of children of foreign workers (Gastarbeiter), and many families vacation abroad. This exposure to outside influences will help them become citizens of the world.

169

169–171. *Fehmarnsund-Brücke, a bridge spanning the channel between the island of Fehmarn and the north German mainland. Considered a major engineering achievement, it is 3213 feet long and 76 feet above the surface of the sea, so that large ships can pass underneath. The island of Fehmarn, a popular resort with a large harbor for yachts and many beaches, is connected by ferryboat with Denmark.*

170

171

173

172, 173. The port of Bremerhaven. Second to Hamburg in terms of size, Bremerhaven is considered one of the world's 'fastest' ports because of its well-designed system of container loading and unloading. One part of the port is in the city of Bremen, connected with the sea and Bremerhaven by the Weser River, navigable even for large vessels.

176. Germany's 5720 miles of navigable waterways, including 1426 miles of canals, play an important role in inland transport. The rivers are linked up by canals, some old and narrow and used only for certain types of cargo — for example, logs transported from wooded areas to industrial centers.

174, 175. Kiel, a lively port on the Baltic Sea chiefly serving ferryboat lines to Scandinavia, is also the main German naval base. Here begins the 61-mile canal between the North Sea and the Baltic, third largest in the world, but first in the frequency of passage — 70,000 ships yearly. Today a modern center of commerce and shipbuilding, the city organizes an annual Kiel Week, a cultural festival with the accent on everything connected with the sea. The sailing events in the 1972 Olympics were held in Kiel.

177.   Holsten Gate (Holstentor)
– a landmark of Lübeck, known as the 'city of marzipan and red wine'. Grapes do not grow in northern Germany but the merchants of Lübeck, long established in the wine trade, developed a taste for the finest French, Italian and Spanish vintages. Marzipan, however, is made here, the boxes bearing a picture of this remarkably fine 16th-century town gate.

178, 179.   Lübeck has entered world literature thanks to 'Buddenbrooks', the novel by Thomas Mann describing his native city and its merchant class. Among its notable buildings are the medieval town hall, reflecting the pride and prosperity of Lübeck, the leading city of the Hanseatic League, and the Protestant church of St Mary completed in 1350. This great Gothic brick church was severely damaged by fire in 1942, but has been superbly restored.

180

180–182. Cuxhaven (Lower Saxony), an important maritime link with Norway, is also a typical North Sea resort. The charms of the North Sea are not those of the Carrribean or Mediterranean: the sea and sky are grey, the water cold. The flat sandy shore is better for long walks along the dunes or horseback riding, breathing the fresh salty air, than for swimming. Even in summer the cool wind discourages sunbathing, except in the shelter of protective awnings.

181

182

183. A wedding in the Protestant church in Worpswede (Lower Saxony). The village has a population of barely 3000, but 300 artists in residence. In the past its internationally-renowned painters' colony included leading German artists such as Overbeck and Vogeler. Apart from the rather gloomy moorland landscape, which seems to appeal to artists, they may have been attracted by local food specialties: products from cattle and pigs grazing peacefully by the sea, and herring, crab and other seafood.

184. Interior of the cathedral in Paderborn (North Rhein-Westphalia), a very ancient city where Charlemagne had a palace. Since 806 there have been churches on the site of the present late Romanesque-Gothic cathedral mostly dating from the 13th century.
185. The interior of Lübeck's Rathaus (town hall). Its construction began in 1226 when Emperor Frederick II awarded Lübeck the privileges of a free city. Over the centuries additions were made: the oldest part, the present south façade, is Gothic, while the major part, including the fine staircase, is in Renaissance style.

186–188. Hohenzollern castle and some of its treasures. The princely Hohenzollern family, from which the castle took its name, goes back to the 10th century. In the 13th it split into its Frankish line, which later adopted the Lutheran faith, and the Swabian line, which remained Catholic. The former produced the electors of Brandenburg, later kings of Prussia and emperors of Germany. The museum in the Schloss displays the Prussian crown of 1889.

188

189. The statue of Roland, 33 feet high, from 1404 on the main square of Bremen is a symbol of civic freedom and independence. The legendary Roland, depicted in epics as one of Charlemagne's most loyal knights, expressed the people's allegiance to the empire rather than to the ruling archibishop, whose men destroyed the previous Roland column on this site. Many other north German towns have similar statues for the same reason.

190. Osnabrück (Lower Saxony): façade of the town hall. From the steps of this late Gothic Rathaus (1487–1505), the Peace of Westphalia was proclaimed in 1648, ending the Thirty Years' War.

191. The lovely Romanesque-Gothic cathedral of Osnabrück has a rich treasury, and Diocesan Museum with works of religious art from the 10th century on. The jeweled cross here is early 14th-century.

191

192

192.   Osnabrück was an early center of Christianity: Charlemagne established a bishopric here c. 780. Its outstanding religious buildings, include its famous cathedral (11th – 16th century) with interesting cloisters.

193.   A room in Osnabrück town hall, in which the Peace of Westphalia was negotiated in 1648, ending thirty years of warfare that devasted Germany and decimated its population.

193

194.   The interior of the Hamburg Rathaus, the largest town hall in Germany, built between 1888 and 1897 in a variety of imitative styles (mostly neo-Renaissance). Since Hamburg is a Land, *the town hall is the seat of its government, though the prime minister here goes by the title of* Bürghermeister *(mayor).*

195, 196.   Berlin – divided into two parts, east and west – suffered the same fate as the country itself. Each half of the city tried to be a showcase for its regime, but there could be no dispute that the western part with its bright lights, well-filled shops, and stylish young people was the more exciting. A not unimportant factor – the cafés and restaurants were definitely superior in the west.

197.   The vast Baroque Charlottenburg palace in Berlin was commissioned in 1695 as the summer residence of Princess Sophie Charlotte, and completed in stages. The massive central section with its dome topped by the figure of Fortuna was finished in 1707.

196

to 'overcome the old conservative social structure', but only in how to achieve this: the Social Democrats still believed in a planned economy, the Christian Democrats in free enterprise. Support for one or the other solution was fairly equal. When West Germany's first postwar parliament voted for its first chancellor, Dr. Konrad Adenauer, leader of the CDU, obtained a majority of only one vote — by voting for himself.

Adenauer took office at the age of seventy-three, a characteristic instance of Germans placing political trust in older men. He wielded so much influence that he could decide even matters like the selection of Bonn as the new capital of West Germany. Many bigger and better known cities, like Munich and Hamburg, competed for the honor; Frankfurt, where kings had been crowned and in 1848 the National Assembly was convened, had the best credentials. But in his Rhöndorf home across the Rhine from Bonn old Adenauer had a rose garden which he liked to cultivate in his spare time. If they wanted him as chancellor, he said, his headquarters would have to be in Bonn. Thus, a small, sleepy town, seat of a venerable university, became the capital of a country that would rise from wartime ruins as one of the most modern and influential in present-day Europe. Adenauer, of course, denies this in his memoirs. He says that he did not wish to go to Frankfurt since the Social Democratic majority in the city might have given the government a different image. This, too, is a good explanation.

The West German economy had the chance to start afresh in 1948 when monetary and economic reforms were carried out practically over-night. Every German received 40 marks, and a month later another 20. The fairness of this measure is debatable, but the fact remains that those who possessed manufacturing facilities or good ideas were able to turn them to a profit very quickly, regardless of the equal start.

In his book *Auf einer Woge von Gold* (On a Wave of Gold), author Kurt Pritzkoleit claims that nine years later, in 1957, there were 3500 millionaires in West Germany, and by 1961 10,000. He cites examples like electronics manufacturer Max Grundig, who started with a patent and the famous 40 marks and ten years later had earned 400 million marks.

At the same time, however, many of the great family fortunes began to dwindle, or the old families at least began to lose control over them. For generations the Krupps had been the wealthiest and most distinguished industrialists in Germany, but in order to survive in a modern economy the state had to come to the aid of the coal and steel empire, and the firm was incorporated. Millionaire families like the Flicks (who controlled Daimler-Benz), the Hortens, Quandts and others sold majority shares of their stocks to major banks. Their playboy descendants relinquished the helm of business for notoriety in the gossip columns and scandal pages of the popular press.

Such privileged individuals aside, most of the German population had to summon up enormous energy and vitality, incredible faith in the future, in order to overcome all the difficulties. Without aid in food from the western countries, people would have starved. Even so, during the first three postwar years the average German consumed only 1300 calories daily, and the black market provided valuable training for those who would later become international businessmen. Strange rules evolved: for example, a sack of rope cost a farmer 330 pounds of wheat, or 440 pounds of rye, or 13 pounds of bacon; for 60 horseshoe nails he had to 'pay' a pound of lard; for 110 pounds of fertilizer, 330 pounds of potatoes, etc. Not surprisingly, having survived in such a jungle of values, the Germans did well in an organized economy. Welcoming order, they

198. *The Kaiser Wilhelm memorial church at the beginning of the Kurfürstendamm, Berlin. Built in 1891–95 in memory of past wars, it was partly destroyed in World War II bombing and deliberately preserved in its ruined state, as a reminder of the horrors of war. So that it could be used as a church, in 1961–63 an extension designed by architect Egon Eiermann was added to the damaged neo-Romanesque part: an octagonal blue glass annex and modern hexagonal tower.*

remained masters of the art of improvisation. Whoever had traded with potatoes, or a box of American or British cigarettes, instead of currency, or could calculate how many ounces of coffee to barter for a pair of nylon stockings, would never be fazed by the stock market.

Economic development in the Federal German Republic, formed from the American, British and French occupation zones, was further bolstered by settled internal and, later, foreign political relations. Keeping an alert watch as the opposition, the Social Democrats saw to it that the CDU, while in power, did not neglect the social welfare aspect of its free market economy policies. And when Willy Brandt and subsequently Helmut Schmidt became chancellor, the conservatives were still strong enough to prevent any excessive left-wing experimentation. The Federal Republic of Germany grew into a model democracy.

One aspect of the 'German miracle' is personified in the figure of Willy Brandt. Born out of wedlock in 1913, his real name was Karl Herbert Frahm, Willy Brandt his political pseudonym. A Social Democrat since 1930, he had to flee the country when Hitler came to power. He was in Spain during the civil war and in Norway when Germany attacked this country, escaping to Sweden. After the war he returned to Germany as a Norwegian diplomat in Norwegian uniform. In political confrontations with him, Adenauer did not shrink from mentioning his illegitimate birth and the fact that he had worn an 'enemy' uniform.

One of the dominant personalities of postwar Germany, Willy Brandt was actually chancellor only from November 1969 until the summer of 1974, when he resigned under obscure circumstances, ostensibly because an East German spy had been discovered working in his entourage. But while in office, as foreign minister before that, and as leader of the Social Democratic Party before and after, he contributed notably to an improved image of Germans in the modern world.

Occasionally a policy that has been pursued for decades can be epitomized by a single gesture. While visiting Warsaw, Brandt, disregarding all protocol, fell to his knees before a war memorial. A man who all his life had actively opposed evil, yet recognized that he was a German, knelt in the name of Germany before the victims of his country's aggression. A gesture like this is more striking and memorable than the fact that the 'eastern policy' which Brandt initiated is now being pursued throughout Europe. Brandt has entered history as that 'nice German', a qualification that reflected on all his compatriots.

The chancellorship was inherited by his party friend, though in many ways opponent in practical politics, Helmut Schmidt, born in 1918. A distinguished economist, he had served in Brandt's government as minister of defence and also economics and finance minister. A pragmatic yet imaginative exponent of a 'social' market economy, he is considered a follower of Erhard's policies, though from the opposing party. This is further evidence of the beneficial consensus of opinion among the leading parties concerning the main outlines of German economic development.

The 'Democratic' Model

While the Federal Republic basked in growing prosperity, the Democratic Republic was generally described as a 'satellite' following Soviet policy. It has often been said that the dismantling of industry was carried out much more rigorously in this part of the country than in the west, but little mention is made of the fact that the East German state had lost its contacts not only with the west, but with the east as well. The Prussian provinces of Silesia, Pomerania, East and West Prussia, and parts of the province of Brandenburg, which before the Second World War had constituted 24 percent of the country's territory, now belonged to Poland or the Soviet Union.

When the war ended, East Germany had 16.7 million inhabitants, the figure rising to 18.7 million in 1947 because of refugees from the east, but by 1961, when the border was more firmly closed and the Berlin wall erected, two million refugees had fled to the west. In the absence of free elections, East Germans were expressing their discontent by 'voting with their feet'.

The entire economy was nationalized, agriculture organized into cooperatives modeled on the Soviet *kolkhoz,* and development geared to five-year plans. While West Germany joined the NATO defence pact and later the European Economic Community (the Common Market), East Germany became a member of the Warsaw pact and its corresponding economic organization, COMECON.

It is interesting that a statistical analysis of the living standard in the two Germanys in the 60s and 70s does not show such marked differences as one might expect. During this period both East and West Germans consumed 3000 calories daily, but mostly carbohydrates and fats in the east. The consumption of coffee, fresh and citrus fruit was double in the west. Per capita purchases of shoes, television sets, radios, movie cameras and kitchen appliances were the same in both Germanys, though quality in the west was superior. West Germans, however, had five times as many cars, East Germans five times as many motorcycles and motor scooters. Every year, every second West German vacationed abroad, while no more than 15 percent of East Germany's inhabitants could afford a foreign holiday, and these almost exclusively in some other Communist country.

In this context it should be mentioned that the German Democratic Republic boasted the highest living standard of all the 'real socialist' countries, with per capita private consumption 50 percent higher than in the Soviet Union.

Firms in the G.D.R. were called *volkseigene Betriebe* ('firms belonging to the people'). The people apparently had little influence, only the state and the omnipresent Communist party, which in the G.D.R. was called the Socialist Unity Party of Germany, formed by the unification, under Soviet pressure, of the Communist and Social Democratic parties. Employees had no special rights regarding management or distribution of income in these 'people's firms'.

Things developed differently in capitalist West Germany, where employers and workers collaborated in a system of co-partnership *(Mitbestimmung)* in several branches of the economy. According to the law on co-partnership in mining and the iron and steel industry, supervisory committees and management had to include an equal number of representatives of the owners and employees. This arrangement proved important when automation was introduced, since steps were taken to avoid the abrupt dismissal of workers, though strikes still broke out, for example, in the graphics industry when printing was computerized. Co-partnership has been introduced in other activities in all companies

Prosperity and Problems

employing more than 20 persons, but mostly in connection with social welfare and personnel policy. In incorporated enterprises, a third of the supervisory committee is comprised of representatives elected by the employees.

The German Federation of Trade Unions is an important factor in the German economy. Every year, union officials sit down with employers in their particular branch to discuss wage contracts, possible pay hikes, shorter working hours. In this way the labor force in West Germany has shared in the nation's increasing wealth, though figures for recent years indicate that employers' incomes have been rising faster than those of their employees. Over the years the unions became very rich institutions, but then made several blunders that did them even more harm politically than financially. The unions were the owners of *Neue Heimat* (New Homeland), the world's largest construction firm, which built and rented out apartments. Mismanagement, however, sent the firm into bankruptcy, and, worse still, it turned out that individual union officials had used the firm to line their own pockets. Its collapse also brought down the powerful *Bank für Gemeinwirtschaft* (Bank for the Public Economy), in which the unions held a majority share. The firm was bailed out by private investors, which suggested to the public that union officials were no substitute for modern entrepreneurs. As a result, the political clout of the unions declined in the late 80s, though still not to be underestimated.

Since the war the West German electorate has steered clear of right-wing or left-wing extremes. From time to time the public became alarmed by the actions of terrorist groups — above all, the brutal murders committed by the Red Army Faction, also known as the Baader-Meinhof Gang — but these had no significant impact on the political and economic situation, even though the targets for assassination were often prominent industrialists and bankers.

Possibly nowhere in the world do people spend so much time and money polishing and pampering their cars as in Germany. The model a person drives often says something about his politics, the way he views the world and life in general. A few lines about the major car manufacturers will therefore not be out of place, especially as automobile production

Food riots in Stettin, 1847, contemporary ink drawing. A century later, Germany again suffered severe food shortages, overcome thanks to foreign aid.

can serve as a good illustration of development in other branches of industry.

Germany's most characteristic major automobile producer is Volkswagen. Few people remember that the prototype for the Volkswagen (the 'people's car') was constructed in 1934 on the express orders of Hitler, who saw mass car-ownership as potentially useful for military purposes. During the war the car was redesigned as a kind of German jeep. Only a third of Volkswagen's facilities survived the war. Deciding that it was not worthwhile to dismantle the remaining plant, British experts concluded: "The vehicle does not meet the basic requirements for a motor-car... too ugly and noisy... commercial production would be quite unprofitable... no competition for British production on the world market." Thus, in 1946 daily output was 30 cars, exclusively for the German market. In 1955 1000 were daily coming off the assembly line, and in late 1960 over 4000. In Europe the ugly, noisy car was affectionately nicknamed the Beetle, in the United States ironically, 'Hitler's baby'. It was to break the world record held by Ford, which had sold 15 million of the Model T 'Tin Lizzies'. When the Beetle was discountinued, the factory produced a worthy successor, the Golf or Rabbit, along with a wide range of other models.

Two large German car manufacturers actually have American owners, who appoint the chief managers and decide on new models. One is Ford, the other Opel, owned by General Motors. Two more big names in the German automobile industry are Daimler-Benz (producing the Mercedes) and BMW, their output less than the afore-mentioned firms but their top-notch quality recognized worldwide. Daimler-Benz has expanded into a mammoth company in which passenger cars represent only one sector of activity. The company has successfully entered the air and space industries, electronics and armaments, believing this to be the only way to compete with American and Japanese industry.

In the late 50s Germany experienced a serious shortage of manpower. For dirtier, unpleasant and comparatively less remunerative jobs, workers poured in from other countries of Europe, from Turkey and North Africa. The highest figure is recorded for 1976, 1,937,134, but together with their families, making six million. Since then the number of *Gastarbeiter* ('guest workers'), as the Germans call them, has declined: in mid-1989 there were 1,689,000 foreign workers employed in West Germany.

Naturally enough, this large influx created as well as solved problems. For example, in the Berlin quarter of Kreuzberg, Turks outnumber Germans. Their traditions and Muslim religious practices keep them apart and arouse protest, especially when unemployment mounts in Germany. On the other hand, with these foreign workers came Italian, Spanish, Yugoslav and Greek restaurants and specialty shops for food that Germans enjoy when traveling in those countries. The government has not allowed Germany to become a land of immigration like the United States. Foreigners cannot participate even in local elections, although they pay the same taxes as their German colleagues. Certain social classes tend to show hostility to foreigners. This is also felt in the eastern part of the country, where foreign labor was recruited in Vietnam and other Asian countries.

To sum up and explain Germany's postwar rise from the ruins to world industrial power, one can do no better than to quote the recipe for success given by Social Democratic economics and finance minister Karl Schiller: "As much competition as possible, as much planning as necessary."

Early Architecture

Art that can be qualified as German begins with the Carolingian empire created by Charlemagne, king of the Franks, in the latter half of the eighth century. As a Christian ruler who recognized the useful unifying and administrative role the Church could play in his vast realm, he did much to strengthen it by his ecclesiastical reforms, establishing schools for the clergy which became centers of learning and art, and building churches, only a handful of which have escaped destruction.

Until then, stone had not been used for construction in the Germanic lands, except by the Romans, who had built temples and palaces, baths and water systems, fortresses and houses of stone, even paving roads with it. The Germans, however, had gone on building their houses of wood. Charlemagne put an end to this, seeking inspiration in the great classical age.

He insisted, however, that his builders should be German, and made Einhard, a Rhinelander, later his biographer, the supervisor of all his building projects. Seeing himself as the 'new Constantine', when he established his capital at Aachen (Aix-la-Chapelle) in 794, he decided to build himself a residence to rival the Great Palace in Constantinople. All that remains of it is the imperial chapel, also intended as Charlemagne's mausoleum, designed by Odo of Metz. Though he clearly relied for inspiration on the church of San Vitale in Ravenna, Odo gave the chapel a heavier, more somber, Germanic aspect, especially evident in the austere westwork that became a characteristic feature of Carolingian and Ottonian architecture. Charlemagne's coronation as emperor took place in Rome five years before the consecration of the chapel in 805, but all his successors until Ferdinand I in 1531 – thirty in number – were crowned here. Although the church was later enlarged to create the present Aachen cathedral, its nucleus, the palatine chapel with its central octagonal area surrounded by eight sturdy pillars, remains unchanged to the present day.

Early German sculpture, inspired by a classical conception of man in a Christian interpretation, first appeared in Aachen as master works by wood carvers and goldsmiths. Examples of their work, and of the magnificent illuminated manuscripts of this age, can be seen in the famous treasury of Aachen cathedral.

The architectural style that developed from that time until the next turning point, at the beginning of the thirteenth century, was not known as Romanesque until the nineteenth century. The name may be misleading because of its associations with peoples speaking Romance languages, for it actually developed in Saxony and Swabia, Bavaria and German Franconia, hence among the Germans.

Some of the old Romanesque churches burned down long ago; others were altered out of all recognition or damaged in the bombing of the Second World War. Among the finest surviving examples are the imperial cathedral in the city of Speyer, consecrated in 1061, and the abbey church in Maria Laach, begun in 1093 but not completed until *c.* 1230. The Romanesque style is monumental; churches were conceived as earthly castles of the kingdom of heaven. Beside architecture, sculpture and painting also flourished. Scope for artistic creativity was likewise found in manuscript illumination, and on textiles: tapestries decorating churches, especially altars, church vestments and the robes of secular rulers. During this period, artists began to compose pictures of multicolored glass in church windows, a technique that appeared for the first time in Romanesque art.

Song and Singers

During the twelfth century a special kind of troubadour poetry called *Minnesang* developed in Germany, influenced by the French *trouvères*, Arabic models, and the much coarser love lyrics of the wandering poets. *Carmina burana* is the title of the oldest collection of love lyrics by itinerant scholars and runaway monks, written down in the thirteenth century in the monastery of Benediktbeuren in Bavaria. (In 1936 they served German composer Carl Orff as the basis for his dramatic oratorio of the same name.)

The creators of the *Minnesang*, the Minnesingers, mainly noblemen, also composed melodies for their love lyrics, which were accompanied by the *Fiedel*, a predecessor of the violin, and the harp. The most celebrated of these lyric poets was Walther von der Vogelweide (probably 1170–1230). On his wanderings from court to court, at the castle of Count Hermann of Thuringia at Wartburg — where much later Luther translated the Bible — he met another great troubadour-poet of his time, Wolfram von Eschenburg. Beside love lyrics, Wolfram wrote what is probably the greatest of the German court epics, *Parzival,* a splendid 28,840-line poem of chivalry. During this period new themes were introduced; apart from religious verse and love lyrics, there were poems with a political or didactic content, and in the villages, realistic, satirical verse. Also at this time the aristocratic Minnesingers were joined by the bourgeois Meistersingers.

With the flourishing of trade and crafts in the medieval German towns, the artisans, organized in guilds, wished to emulate the aristocracy and in their own way continue the troubadour tradition. The Meistersingers were poets and composers as well as trained singers. Work in the Meistersinger associations ('song schools') reflected guild practices. Just as apprentices had to go through preparatory stages before they could attain the coveted rank of *Meister,* the rules of the Nuremberg school of singers had similar provisions: "He who cannot read notes without error is a pupil; if he knows them perfectly, he is a friend; if he knows at least five or six melodies, he is a singer; if he writes words for a given melody, he is a poet; if he composes a new melody, he is a master." At singing contests a special duty was given to 'markers' *(Merker),* who recorded mistakes, very much like judges at figure-skating competitions. In some cities such contests aroused as much public excitement and intense rivalry as major sporting events today.

The greatest of the Meistersingers was a shoemaker from Nuremberg, Hans Sachs (1494–1576). His carnival plays, satires, short lyric or

199. *German products are known for their quality throughout the world. The phrase 'made in Germany' is considered a guarantee of excellence, a reputation due primarily to the reliability of the German labor force. The term for a skilled worker or artisan – der Meister – is a title of respect.*

religious verses have none of the rigidity and uniformity that characterize much of his colleagues' work; he criticized the Catholic clergy and aristocracy, but also the 'dumb peasants'. He sided actively with Martin Luther – an early example of a 'politically engaged' artist. Richard Wagner used him as the principal character in his opera, *Die Meister-singer von Nürnberg*, in which he censures the obstinate use of traditional models, pedantry, and ignorance of the essential purpose of art: to be a part of life.

Martin Luther (1483–1546) had a decisive impact not only on religious and political life in Germany, but on art as well, above all literature and music. "I am not pleased with those who despise music," he wrote. "Music is a talent and a gift of God, not of man. With music one forgets anger, filth, arrogance and other vices. After theology, I give music second place, and the greatest honor." He introduced congregational hymn singing into Protestant services, and all Lutheran churches had to employ a cantor to direct the church music. It should be mentioned, however, that more 'radical' Protestants considered music godless and vain. For example, Ulrich Zwingli (1484–1531) ordered church organs destroyed and banned singing during services.

Luther, for his part, proposed that religious texts should be written for certain secular melodies, commenting that 'the devil should not have all the beautiful tunes'. Luther himself wrote the words of several hymns that are still in regular use, and in this way helped to shape the modern German literary language. As he said, "One should listen to the way one's mother speaks at home, how children speak in the street, ask a simple man at the market, then write down what they say." Beside pamphlets and theological treatises, Luther wrote fairy-tales and collected folk sayings, but his greatest contribution to the German language was his translation of the Bible. Thanks to Gutenberg's invention of printing by movable type, Luther's Bible and other writings were widely available wherever the German language was spoken. Catholics, however, were forbidden even to pick it up. As a modern German writer, Johannes Gross, puts it, "The German literary language was predominantly the possession of the Protestants... If we exlude the converts of the Romantic school, who also sprang from certain Protestant trends of enlightenment, until the nineteenth century the major German authors include only three Catholics: Eichendorff, Stifter and Grillparzer."

From Gothic to Baroque

200. *Fertile wheat fields near Vohburg on the Danube. It is a misconception that Germany is exclusively an industrial country, its skies thick with soot from smoking chimneys, steel mills and factories. Germany not only feeds its population, but owing to state support for farmers, now exports food products.* ▷

Even before the period of Romanesque architecture ended in Germany, the Gothic was already in full flower in France, where it originated around the middle of the twelfth century. The cathedral in Magdeburg (1219), destroyed during the Second World War, was the first to adopt the French method of construction. For the cathedral in Cologne, Germany's most celebrated example of Gothic church architecture, the foundation stone was laid in 1248. Beside churches, the prospering bourgeoisie also built town halls in this style, for example, in Lübeck, Aachen, Braunschweig and Munich, competing with the courts and castles of the nobility. The late Gothic remained popular in Germany during the Renaissance, when the Italian influence on architecture was noticeable but not too strong. Outstanding buildings from this period are the palace at Aschaffenburg, and town halls in Leipzig, Bremen and Augsburg. While building in stone and brick, the Germans retained their love of wood and graced their towns with attractive half-timbered *(Fachwerk)* buildings.

202

201, 202. Eastern Germany has always been less affluent than the western part. Decades of 'real socialism' in the G.D.R. further deepened the difference in living standards between them, though not necessarily always to the advantage of the West. In less developed regions, neighbors are more likely to lend a helping hand, for example, when a thatched roof needs fixing — warm, friendly relations that are disappearing in cities.

203. In the villages (this is
Ahrenshoop) cows are still turned
loose to graze at will, not
spending their lives tied to
feeders, turning them into milk-
and-meat-producing machines.
Yet modern life has its own
requirements – farm animals have
to give part of their barn space to
man's new friend, the car.

204

204, 205. Repairs on the road to
Apold in eastern Germany. The
name of this town is recorded in
literature thanks to Goethe.
Principal minister of state in the
small duchy of Weimar, he noted
in his diary: 'in nearby Apold the
weavers are starving.' More than
200 years ago Apold already had
a manufacturing industry and
social problems, unsolved by the
socialist society glorified in the
mural.

207

206–208. Vast estates were once characteristic of eastern Germany, which is in general more rural. The landowners belonging to the Prussian aristocracy were called Junkers. When the new authorities expropriated land after the Second World War and set up cooperatives, agriculture did not progress as expected. Returning all this nationalized land, worked by others for decades, to the heirs of its former owners will pose problems for a united Germany.

208

209

209–211. The senior citizens resting on a bench in the park in Lützen are certainly not thinking about the great battle that took place here in 1632 when Swedish King Gustavus Adolphus was killed fighting Count Wallenstein during the Thirty Years' War. This tranquil area near Leipzig is perhaps the part of Germany that has changed least over the past few centuries. Its inhabitants, renowned for their obstinacy, were the first to accept the teachings of their compatriot Martin Luther (born in nearby Eisleben) and Protestantism.

210

211

212

213

212–214. *What might people in Leipzig
(opposite) be talking about? Unification has
not automatically brought equality.
Earnings in the country's western part are
several times higher, while prices in the
east are rapidly rising. Much work is still
done in obsolete, inefficient ways, and
a certain time-warp charm cannot
compensate for lack of modern amenities.*

215

216

215–217. One of the greatest
opportunities for farmers in the eastern
part of Germany is the production of
organic food in natural conditions. Though
air pollution in certain industrial sectors is
even worse than in the west, for ecology
was not a major concern, many crystal-
clear streams hold promise of a good catch
and the flock of free-range geese will
certainly provide healthy meat.

The Baroque in German architecture is well illustrated by palaces in Berlin and Dresden. After the Thirty Years' War many Italian architects came to work in Germany again, bringing some of their ideas. The Rococo is best exemplified in Bavarian church interiors and the palaces of Frederick the Great in Charlottenburg and Potsdam.

The greatest painter, art theoretician and, above all, engraver to emerge from the late Gothic tradition was Albrecht Dürer of Nuremberg (1471–1528). The son of a goldsmith, Dürer retained many of the qualities of the craftsman: his woodcuts and copperplate engravings remain unsurpassed. He wrote treatises on the perfect proportions of the human image and immediately demonstrated by painting Adam and Eve. Thematically, his work is endlessly diverse: ranging from mythological and biblical themes, landscapes and architecture, to faithful renderings of plants and animals. Thanks to several fine self-portraits, we know exactly what he looked like at different periods of his life. He also portrayed many distinguished contemporaries, among them Emperor Maximilian I, who paid him an annual salary from 1515 on.

Dürer's contemporaries included Lucas Cranach and Hans Holbein. Lucas Cranach the Elder (1472–1553), considered the founder of the Danubian school of painting (Donauschule), was among the first to combine human figures and landscapes, that is, to depict people in a natural setting. He obtained so many commissions he set up a workshop where his sons, Hans and Lucas the Younger, painted under his guidance. In the Holbein family it was exactly the reverse. The senior Hans Holbein (1465–1524) was less famous than his son, Hans Holbein the Younger (1497–1543). Born in Augsburg, Germany, he learned his trade from his father and then moved to Switzerland, ending up as court painter to Henry VIII in London, where he died. Shaking off the late Gothic influence more easily than Dürer, Hans Holbein was a true representative of the Renaissance.

With the death of these masters, the fine arts in Germany entered a decline. The Baroque and Classicist periods did not produce painters of comparable stature and international renown.

Music in Germany, however, was a very different story. Until the sixteenth century, church singing was not accompanied by musical instruments; then organ music began to gain favor. Virtuoso organists like Dietrich Buxtehude (1637–1701), Franz Tunder (1614–1667) and Johann Pachelbel (1635–1706), in a sense the predecessors of Bach, were masters of technique and artistry. With the appearance of Handel and Bach, German music could hold its own among its European neighbors.

Georg Friedrich Handel (Händel) and Johann Sebastian Bach were born the same year, 1685, and not far from each other – Handel in Halle and Bach in Eisenach. Bach died in 1750 in Leipzig and Handel in 1759 in London. The first composer to make money from his music, Handel was lionized during his lifetime. In contrast, Bach's genius was recognized by few of his contemporaries. He lived simply, almost in indigence, as church musician, organist and choirmaster to the courts of petty rulers. His large opus, now acclaimed as the crowning point of Baroque music, included over 200 cantatas, the Passions according to St. John and St. Matthew, masses and motets, preludes and fugues, toccatas for organ, piano and lute, chamber and orchestral music. Handel, on the other hand, showed a preference for operas and oratorios, instrumental pieces and compositions for large orchestras. Though born only 28 days and 60 miles apart, these two musical geniuses never met.

The first performance of a German opera was given in the castle of

218. *Eastern Germany boasts large, beautiful forests and unspoilt scenery that the Germans of the west are now discovering after unification. The province of Thuringia abounds in romantic landscapes while the mountains of Saxony are called the 'Saxon Switzerland'.*

Torgau in 1627. It was entitled *Daphne* and written by oratorio composer Heinrich Schütz (1585–1672), who succeeded in reconciling the new Italian musical form with German tradition. In the second half of the seventeenth century, the prosperous mercantile city of Hamburg founded an opera house to compete with the performances being given in the residences of the German princes. The city music director was Georg Philipp Telemann (1681–1767), who wrote 40 operas and started the first German music journal, *Der getreue Music-Meister* (The True Music Master).

Weimar and the Golden Age

The eighteenth century also saw the emergence of German writers in the forefront of the European literary scene. It is strange that two of the greatest figures in all German literature should have been contemporaries who lived in the same small place. During the second half of the eighteenth century the German province of Thuringia comprised 27 mini-states, one of them the duchy *(Herzogtum)* of Weimar. When Johan Wolfgang Goethe (1749–1832) arrived in November 1776, the town had less than 6000 inhabitants, but the small ducal residence became a 'court of the muses'. Beside Goethe, who remained here for the rest of his life as president of the duke's secret council, i.e. prime minister, a kind of minister of culture, finance and economics, and also for a long time director of the ducal theater, Weimar was home to another great personality in German letters, Friedrich Schiller (1759–1805). These two poets, very different in their work and approach to life, were united in close friendship and support for one another.

Goethe and Schiller wrote most of their works in Weimar, and their plays were staged here. In the first performance of *Iphigenie auf Tauris* (1787), Goethe himself acted one of the parts, the two friends directing it together. All of Germany, and soon other centers of culture further afield, kept their eyes fixed on the little duchy. Through a turbulent new movement known as *Sturm und Drang* ('Storm and Stress') they introduced German literature to a brilliant period of classicism. Their vast opus includes virtually every literary genre and some of the world's supreme literary works: their ballad poetry; Goethe's *Werther*, a landmark in the development of the novel; his masterpiece *Faust*, which defies classification; his magnificent novel *Wilhelm Meister*; Schiller's tragedies such as *Maria Stuart*, *The Maid of Orleans*, and *William Tell*, superior to all other European drama of the age.

Naturally there were influential writers before the Weimar classical period in Germany. The celebrated critic and pioneer dramatist Gotthold Ephraim Lessing (1729–1781), the first German to take a serious interest in Shakespeare, was also a student of the ancient Greek writers. His writings on dramaturgy are still fundamental to an understanding of classical tragedy. Also associated with Weimar is the scholarly investigation and recording of oral literature, most notably by the Grimm brothers.

Five decades, roughly from 1780 to 1830, were supremely important for German ideas. Classicism was succeeded by the Romantic school and the great philosophers. This was the time of Kant, Hegel, Schelling and Fichte, Hamann and Schopenhauer. Apart from Goethe and Schiller, notable writers included Herder and Wieland, Kleist and Hölderin, the strange musician and satirist, E. Th. A. Hoffmann, and soon the ironic Heinrich Heine. Rahel Varnhagen conducted a political and literary salon in Berlin, gathering the finest intellects of the period, and women began to take a more active part in cultural activities.

This was likewise a period of great advances in science and scholarship, coupled with the growth of the German universities. Humboldt reformed higher education; the mathematician Gaus, astronomer Frunhofer, historian Ranke, and theologian Schleiermacher were all active. Suddenly it seemed that the influences of England, France and Italy were no longer dominant. Now that the Germans were contributing to world civilization, Goethe first used the expression 'world literature'. At the same time Bach's music was rediscovered and properly assessed; Mozart, Beethoven, Schubert and Mendelssohn were composing.

Strangely enough, though a united German *Reich* did not exist, and the small German states were of negligible importance, especially after the defeats inflicted by Napoleon, the German spirit triumphed, as if trying to prove that statehood was superfluous. In his book about the Germans, Johannes Gross writes: "This was a great time for Germany. Without any politics, indeed in opposition to politics, Germany suddenly acquired a unified literary culture, a consensus of opinion prevailed in philosophical, literary enlightenment. This was a time when everyone in Germany wrote good German — strong, clear, natural, cultivated, and often elegant." It is no exaggeration to say that ever since then the German sense of identity has rested on that golden age.

True, medieval German philosophers had made a notable contribution to European ideas: Albertus Magnus (1206–1280) founded Aristotelian scholasticism, and Meister Eckhart (1260–1327) speculative mysticism. But after the Middle Ages, other cultures advanced much more rapidly. Viewed from London or Paris, both Immanuel Kant (1724–1804), who never left his distant Köningsberg, somewhere near the Russian border, and Georg Friedrich Hegel (1770–1831), who at least taught at the university of Berlin, capital of the small Prussian state still recovering from the passage of Napoleon's troops, were both denizens of remote provinces. Nevertheless, they had a better understanding of the essence and meaning of the world than any other philosophers of their time. Though many details of their teachings are now considered obsolete, Kant's transcendental idealism, Hegel's concept of dialectics, have been a tremendous force in the history of philosophy, penetrating nearly every pore of modern thought.

In this golden age of German music, it is difficult, and indeed unnecessary, to separate the composers of Germany from those of Austria, which at that time figured as one of the large German states. The best illustration of this is the career of Ludwig van Beethoven, who was born in 1770 in Bonn and died in 1827 in Vienna. Alongside native-born Austrians Joseph Haydn (1732–1809) and Wolfgang Amadeus Mozart (1756–1791), this Rhinelander forms part of the great Viennese trio of classics. Then comes another tragic musical genius who died young, Vienna-born Franz Schubert (1798–1828), succeeded by other outstanding musicians: the Austrian Anton Bruckner (1824–1896), Johannes Brahms (1833–1897), born in Hamburg but also attracted to Vienna, the renowned pianist Clara Schumann from Leipzig (1819–1896) and her brilliant husband Robert Schumann, born in Zwickau (1810–1856).

For his work to be performed and appreciated, a composer required a wealthy patron and the cultivated public of a glittering metropolis. This explains why so many German musicians were drawn to Vienna, like moths to a flame. The exception was Richard Wagner (1813–1883), who enjoyed the lavish patronage of King Ludwig of Bavaria.

Baron Wilhelm von Humboldt (1767–1835), philologist, diplomat and writer, who played a major role in the founding of Berlin University (1809).

Repression, Revolt and Flux

In connection with the French Revolution, the elderly Goethe declared, "All apostles of liberty have always been repugnant to me..." His friend Schiller, ten years younger, was considered more revolutionary, but after his youthful work *The Robbers*, the revolutionary action in Schiller's tragedies takes place in England, Spain, Switzerland, far from the German states. To his line in *Don Carlos*, "Sire, grant freedom of thought!" the public would react much later, for at the time ordinary people did not spend too much time thinking, and rulers placed little restraint on the intellectual élite who did, seeing no danger in this activity. A change in their attitude, and that of German writers, came with the approach of revolutionary 1848. One of the best examples is Heinrich Heine (1797–1856), a great poet but also a remarkable political satirist, acquainted with Karl Marx. As a young man Heine had gone to pay his respects to the aging Goethe, but it was obviously not a meeting of minds.

Born a few years after Heine, Georg Büchner was only twenty-four years old when he died (1837), before Heine became a revolutionary. This brilliant young man, who by the age of twenty had written three plays (including *The Death of Danton*), laid the foundations for modern drama with his pamphlet *Der Hessische Landbote* (roughly translatable as 'country courier from Hesse'), in which he attacked the rich, the bourgeoisie and 'feudal mini-states' *(Feudale Kleinstaaterie)* no less vigorously than Marx and Engels would do a whole decade later in their *Communist Manifesto*. Heine had to flee Germany for France, just as Marx and Engels left for England. It was now difficult for thinkers of international stature to remain in Germany.

Poet Johann Christian Friedrich Hölderlin (1770–1843) did not escape abroad but into insanity. For more that half his life his soul, as the Germans would say, was in complete darkness. Friedrich Nietzsche (1844–1900) also spent the last ten years of his life in an asylum for the insane. Though much better known as a philosopher, Nietzsche also wrote lyrical verse and stands in a sense on the threshold of modern German poetry. His idea of the Superman *(Übermensch)* was later usurped by Hitler, whose ultra-nationalistic views of the world Nietzsche himself would have despised. This abuse of his work caused progressive-minded people throughout the world to turn against everything the philosopher wrote, as they did against Wagner's music, which Nietzsche originally appreciated and later condemned. His best works, *Thus Spake Zarathustra* and *Beyond Good and Evil*, were written in such powerful, persuasive prose that, before the period of disillusionment, they exerted a wide influence. One thing is certain, however: what we today call the German spirit cannot be imagined without Friedrich Nietzsche.

The closer one draws to the present, the more difficult it becomes to select from the great choral symphony of German culture — its art, literature, music, painting, theater and film — the voices that deserve special attention. The world has become smaller, communications technology allows both man and his ideas and artefacts to travel faster, generating possibilities of reciprocal influence, a more cosmopolitan approach to the world. Furthermore, history seems to have quickened its step. An important German writer like Gerhart Hauptmann (1862–1946) lived through four completely different periods of his country's history, experiencing in a single lifetime changes that in the past would have taken centuries. In imperial Germany Hauptmann was known as a socially progressive writer whose plays, for example, *The Weavers*, were committed to the struggle for human and social rights. He received the Nobel Prize in 1921. At the beginning of the First World War he became an

Heinrich Heine (1797–1856), one of the greatest German lyric poets and an outstanding satirist.

enthusiastic German nationalist. During the Weimar republic, he wrote less and made more appearances, trying to emulate Goethe, yet accepted an invitation from Maxim Gorki and signed an appeal against hunger. During Hitler's rule he even agreed to serve as president of the Academy of Literature, which expelled all members with liberal views or of Jewish descent. Hauptmann lived to see Soviet troops enter Germany and allowed himself to be glorified by the Communists. So many times in his life he switched with ease, perhaps unconsciously, from one side to another. If a great writer could behave like this, could one expect more from his people?

A similar figure was composer Richard Strauss (1864–1949). He, too, was honored under all regimes; his operas *Salome* and *Elektra* and the operetta *Der Rosenkavalier* were acclaimed a high point in German music. But his vacillation and inconsistency in both music and public life prompted the comment, "If it's Richard – I'll take Wagner, if it's Strauss – I'll take Johann."

Expressionism and Experiment

Early in the twentieth century German painting again began to attract notice. Between 1911 and 1914, an association of avant-garde painters called *Der Blaue Reiter* (the Blue Rider) was active in Munich. The name of the group, which was to exert an enormous influence on art, was taken from a painting by Wassily Kandinsky (1866–1944), a Russian who had come to Germany in 1896. The innovative school of architectural design known as the *Bauhaus*, as well as German expressionist and abstract art, all developed from the ideas of this group.

Among the best known of the *Blaue Reiter* expressionists was Swiss-born Paul Klee (1879–1940), and among the abstract artists Franz Marc (born in 1880, killed in the war in 1916). Other eminent figures in the group were Macke, Beckman and Kokoschka, while guest contributors to their major exhibitions included such names as Picasso, Malevich, Braque and Vlaminck.

Expressionism was also of importance in literature. Immediately following the First World War, an anthology was published entitled *Twilight of Mankind,* obviously an allusion to the Twilight of the Gods. Its editor, Kurt Pinthaus, selected the most outstanding poets of the period, some of whom later sided with the Nazis, others with the Communists. Thus, Gottfried Benn (1886–1956), physician and lyricist, first supported Hitler and then, allegedly disillusioned, withdrew from politics by becoming an army medical officer, while Johannes Becher (1891–1958) fled to the U.S.S.R. and after the Second World War even became East German minister of culture.

Often listed among the expressionists is Franz Kafka (1883–1924), though his work is so distinctive it may require special qualification. Like many other major German-language writers, Kafka was born in Prague. He came from a Jewish family, worked for an insurance company, and published several short stories that aroused interest among a small circle of readers. After his early death from tuberculosis, his friend Max Broder did not execute the terms of his will and burn his manuscripts. His novels *The Castle* and *The Trial,* the latter not even finished, were posthumously published and established Kafka as one of the outstanding novelists of the century. Never has man's isolation and search for meaning in a hostile world been more vividly conveyed, but Kafka only asked questions without any hope of finding the answers. Politically he was uncommitted, for he did did not believe that either Marxism or the bourgeois society offered a satisfactory solution. Some critics claim that he foresaw the horrors of the Fascist concentration camps. As an interpretation this would be an oversimplification; he was actually depicting the horrors of our everyday life.

Another writer who lived and worked outside the mainstream of contemporary literary trends and artistic circles was the greatest German lyric poet of the century, Rainer Maria Rilke (1875–1926). He, too, was born in Prague, like the expressionist playwright, novelist and poet Franz Werfel (1890–1954), whose novel *Musa Dagh* about the genocide of the Armenians in Turkey anticipated the Holocaust, or the brilliant journalist Egon Erwin Kisch (1885–1948). But while Kafka, Werfel and Kisch were Jews, Rilke came from an Austro-German family of civil servants, and even tried to pass himself off as an aristocrat. Introducing new rhythms and rhymes, he breathed fresh life into German poetry. Unlike his expressionist contemporaries, he sought beauty and transparent symbolism. It is of interest that one of his great loves was Lou Andreas Salome, who had close relationships with Friedrich Nietzsche and Sigmund Freud. (Another remarkable woman who shared the lives of several artists was Alma Mahler Werfel. First married to the composer Gustav Mahler, she became the mistress of Oskar Kokoschka and of the founder of the *Bauhaus* group, architect Walter Gropius, and finally the wife of Franz Werfel, whom she survived.)

Mann and Brecht

Among the scores of writers representing twentieth-century Germany, Thomas Mann (1875–1955) and Bertolt Brecht (1898–1956) have been particularly influential abroad.

The son of a wealthy merchant from Lübeck, Thomas Mann was the best known of a whole family of writers. His elder brother Heinrich (1871–1950), made a name for himself with his novel about the German middle class, *Professor Unrat*. Its screen version entitled *The Blue Angel* became a cult film for generations of moviegoers, not least because of sultry, long-legged Marlene Dietrich. Also writers of distinction are his daughter Erika and sons, novelist Klaus and historian Golo. Thomas Mann was awarded the Nobel Prize in 1929 for his portrayal of nineteenth-century bourgeois society in *Buddenbrooks*, the lengthy novel which was his first great success. Other major works that are read in translation around the world include *Death in Venice, The Magic Mountain,* the four-part novel *Joseph and His Brothers,* and *Felix Krull.* In his novel *Dr. Faustus,* he tried to analyze the German mind and character confronted with the forces of Fascism, and at the same time explain Arnold Schönberg's dodecaphonic technique of composition. Combining tradition with modernity, his works appeal equally to highbrows and the general reading public.

Thomas Mann left for the United States when the National Socialists came to power. One of the most distinguished German emigrants, he opposed Hitler in his writing and radio appearances. In this respect Bertolt Brecht was his ally. Otherwise, these two great contemporaries had little in common apart from mutual antipathy and lack of appreciation for the other as an artist. They certainly did not see eye to eye on politics, for Brecht was a committed, if unorthodox, Communist.

Born into to a well-to-do family of paper manufacturers, Brecht was a gifted poet, and wrote short stories and novels, but his fame rests on his work for the stage. Not since Molière and Shakespeare had there been such a versatile man of the theater: playwright, director, administrator and organizer, theoretician and originator of new ideas on dramaturgy. After his first rebellious expressionist plays of the 1920s in Munich, he became dramatist for the inventive director, Erwin Pascator, in Berlin. *The Threepenny Opera*, with music by Kurt Weil, staged in 1928 in Berlin, brought him fame and fortune. Poking fun at middle-class values, he claimed it was a greater crime to found a bank than to rob one, but people still applauded. He emigrated in 1933 and his most mature plays were written abroad: *Mother Courage, The Good Woman of Setzuan, The Caucasian Chalk Circle* and *The Life of Galileo*, which had its first performance (with Charles Laughton playing the lead) in the United States, where Brecht lived from 1941. After the war he was summoned before the Congressional Committee for Un-American Activities and had to leave the United States, moving in 1948 to East Germany, where he was assigned a theater for his experimental work and founded the famous Berliner Ensemble. For the most part, he did not criticize the regime, but just to be on the safe side he took out Austrian citizenship. On one occasion he ironically commented, "With great concern I have learned how dissatisfied our government is with the people. Why doesn't it elect another people?"

That Brecht as the leading personality in the German theater should enjoy in a Communist state all the freedom of at least a highly favored court jester is an indication of how much this form of art is appreciated in Germany. The Germans had adopted Schiller's dictum that the theater is an 'institution of morality'. In the late 1980s West Germany had 140 theaters serving a population of about 60 million, 80 of them public, i.e. subsidized by the state or city, while East Germany with its much smaller population of around 16 million had 112 state-subsidized theaters.

The same support was given to museums and public galleries exhibiting the works of painters and sculptors, to orchestras ranging from philharmonics to chamber ensembles. In the realm of the arts Germany, even divided, attained a status appropriate to its economic might and cultural heritage.

The world's biggest book fair is held every October in Frankfurt, mecca of publishers, printers, booksellers and literary agents. Amid the hubbub of copyright negotiations, many German names can be heard. The most distinguished and widely translated German writers since the Second World War include novelist Heinrich Böll (1917–1985), Nobel-award winner, longtime president of the international P.E.N. Club and a tireless human rights advocate, and Günter Grass, born in 1927, best known for his novel *The Tin Drum*.

'Portait of Anna Meyer' by Hans Holbein the Younger, pastel, c.1520.

Cinematography

German artists and technicians have played a major role in the development of cinematography. In 1895, when the Lumière brothers gave the first public showings of their films in Lyon, Skadanowski and Mester did the same in Berlin. Several years before Hollywood, in 1922, Vogt, Engel and Masolle experimented with talking pictures in Germany, but their idea of accompanying silent films with phonograph records proved a commercial failure.

Somewhat unusually, the founder of the German film industry was the army. In 1917, the High Command financed the setting up of the UFA company, hoping to use it for propaganda films. Just after the war, in

219. The royal hunting lodge at Moritzburg, one of the most beautiful Baroque castles in eastern Germany, located northwest of Dresden. Originally built for the aristocratic Wettin family (1524–1546), it was renovated between 1722 and 1730 by the noted architect M. D. Pöppelmann, who was employed by Saxon rulers and designed several outstanding buildings for them. Moritzburg now houses a world-famous museum of Baroque art.

1919, Robert Wienes made *Dr Caligari's Cabinet,* one of the early masterpieces of world film. Theoreticians would later claim that in the fictional tyrant, Caligari, Wienes foreshadowed Hitler. A similarly horrific type is *Dr Mabuse,* created in 1922 by one of the greatest directors, Fritz Lang.

From the beginning German film-makers, much more than American, relied on literature for their subjects. The first 'epic' film, in every sense of the word, with its great crowd scenes, was Lang's *Nibelungen* (1924), based on the medieval epic poem of that name. A major place in film history belongs to the celebrated theater and film director Max Reinhardt (1873–1943), an Austrian by birth, who spent his last ten years working in Hollywood, where he established a school for actors and directors. As early as 1913, in his *One Night in Venice,* he shook off theatrical conventions and invented some typical 'filmic effects'. Thanks to Reinhardt, many of the leading German writers and actors of the 20s were eager to work for the cinema.

Many other prominent German film-makers beside Lang and Reinhardt emigrated to America for political, artistic or financial reasons. One such was Ernst Lubitsch (1892–1947), who made one of the first high-budget films in Germany, *Madame Dubarry* (1919), and went on to become head of production at Hollywood's Paramount Studios.

The Blue Angel, perhaps the most successful German film of all time, was also inspired by a literary work (Heinrich Mann's novel *Professor Unrat*), but owes its fame more to the performances of Marlene Dietrich and Emil Jannings, and the masterly direction of Josef von Sternberg.

Both Dietrich and Sternberg joined the growing German colony in Hollywood, but even during the Nazi period, the national cinematography, under the auspices of Goebbels, produced some works of artistic merit, although, as was the case with *Jew Süss,* they served propaganda aims – here, anti-Semitic. Oddly enough, the literary work that was exploited on film for this purpose was written by a German Jew, the distinguished novelist Lion Feuchtwanger, who was exiled in 1933.

In the 60s, the film industry took on a fresh lease of life when the 'New German Cinema' was born.

Volker Schlöndorff, one of its leading lights, continued the tradition of filming works by major contemporary writers: *The Lost Honor of Katarina Blum* was based on a novella by Heinrich Böll, and *The Tin Drum* on the Günter Grass novel. Another eminent director in this group, Wim Wenders, made a series of notable films in collaboration with the prominent writer Peter Handke. Probably the best known of this generation of directors is Rainer Werner Fassbinder, now a cult figure, whose powerful films are as dark and depressing as his own life story and tragic early death. *The Bitter Tears of Petra von Kant, Maria Braun's Marriage* and *Lilly Marleen* are among the most successful of his many pictures. This same German 'new wave' also carried several fine women directors, such as Margarethe von Trott and Döris Dörrie, to the forefront of German cinematography.

The intellectual, in the modern sense of the word, was born in Germany after the French Revolution, but actually began to play his present role only after the Second World War. Before this, even to such a mind as philosopher Hegel, the state was an exalted, moral entity, a totality above all individuals. It took the fearful abuses committed by Hitler's state to bring about a fundamental change of attitude, with the result that at least in West Germany the voices of intellectuals, writers and artists, came to serve as a more important political counterweight than any other form of opposition.

220. Architect Pöppelmann's masterpiece is the Zwinger palace in Dresden, which Duke August the Strong had built for court festivities (1711–1722). It originally had three wings enclosing a large courtyard; the fourth side, an art gallery, was added in 1847. Severely damaged in wartime bombing, the Zwinger has been completely restored and now again houses its priceless collection of paintings, notably Italian old masters. ▷

221

221. Dresden, often called 'Florence on the Elbe', is considered one of the loveliest cities in all Germany. Much of the credit goes to the Saxon electoral princes, later kings, who were not only wealthy but sufficiently enlightened to assemble the finest architects and art works. The large mural in the picture, 'Expedition of the Electors', does honor to the rulers responsible for Dresden's beauty.

222. Statues of the great German poet, Johann Wolfgang Goethe, are scattered the length and breadth of the country. There is one in Leipzig as well (above), though he spent much less time here than in nearby Weimar.

JOHANN
SEBASTIAN
BACH

223. Monument to Johann Sebastian Bach, regarded by many as Germany's greatest composer, stands before the church of St Thomas in Leipzig. Bach's life and work were closely linked with this city and church, where he was employed as cantor.

225

224, 225. While Dresden was a city of palaces, kings and aristocrats, Leipzig was a predominantly middle-class community of merchants and artisans. Since early times it has been a center of book and music publishing, and noted for its fairs. The efforts of the prosperous burghers to rival the grander folk of nearby Dresden are reflected in its architecture and monuments.

226

228

226–232. The image Germans present to the world has undoubtedly changed in recent decades. Once seen as militaristic and belligerant, today they are much more open to the world than most nations. Few foreigners are aware of the marked regional differences between them, but the Germans feel them strongly. In eastern Germany, for example, the Saxons in the south consider themselves easygoing and cheerful compared to the Prussians up north.

229

230

231

232

233

233.   The town hall of Meissen. At the
time of the powerful Saxon electors and
kings, the method of making porcelain,
previously known only to the Chinese, was
discovered by chance near here, by
alchemists employed by the ruler to find
a way of making gold. Meissen china,
produced here since the early 18th
century, has long been world famous,
though it is more commonly known as
Dresden china.

234.   In front of the theater in Weimar stands a joint monument to the writers Goethe and Schiller, who spent a large part of their lives in this city and staged many of their plays for the first time in this very theater. In the 1919–1933 period, Germany was often referred to as the 'Weimar republic', in reference to the fact that the first republican parliament was convened in this theater.

235

236

235–237. *Rostock with its large shipyards is the biggest port in eastern Germany. An ancient center of commerce in the Baltic, it joined the Hanseatic League in the 14th century. Because of its port installations and Heinkel aircraft factory, it was heavily bombed in World War II, but has retained or rebuilt much that is of architectural interest.*

238. Leipzig, which enjoyed pride of place among the cities of East Germany because of its industry and trade fairs, will be remembered as the scene of the first large-scale demonstrations against the G.D.R. regime in the autumn of 1989.

239. Life moved at a slower pace in East Germany. The citizens of the Federal Republic, according to statistics from the early 80s, had five times as many cars in proportion to the population as their fellow Germans in the east, though the latter had five times as many bicycles and motorcycles.

240. Naumburg, a town in the Saale valley in eastern Germany (pop. 40,000). The medieval town suffered several serious fires, the last in 1532, after which a new town arose with fine mansions and a Renaissance town hall, which have survived. Of the fortifications built during the wars against the Poles, only Mary's Gate (1446) still stands. Once a thriving Hanseatic city, Naumburg declined after the rise of Leipzig.

HISTORIC CITIES

Berlin

The most impressive approach to Berlin (pop. 3,353,000) is by plane, landing preferably at Schönefeld airport in the eastern sector. Approaching the other international airport, Tegel, in the middle of the western part, the pilot must guide his jet so low past tall buildings that the passenger is filled more with anxiety than pleasure at the view. But coming into Schönefeld, one can see how two rivers, the Spree and the Havel, intersect the forty-mile-wide city and link up with a network of canals and lakes around it and within its very perimeter. An aerial view also clearly shows how the now demolished wall cut across streets, leaving large gashes in the urban fabric.

It is not even six miles from the opera in East Berlin, on the city's proudest avenue, Unter den Linden, past the Brandenburg Gate and along ruler-straight boulevards to the opera in West Berlin. Although the strictly-controlled border checkpoints have gone, because of dense traffic it can still take nearly an hour to drive between these two points. Fortunately the main thoroughfares, subway, and renowned *S-Bahn* are connected, making it easy to get from one part of the city to another.

Compared with many other major European cities, Berlin is relatively young, having recently celebrated is 800th anniversary. In the thirteenth century, the site was occupied by two settlements, Berlin and Kölln (not to be confused with the much older Köln on the Rhine). These two communities merged but did not really begin to grow until after the Thirty Years' War. Prussian King Frederick William I surrounded his capital with a wall in 1734, a time when other cities were pulling down their fortifications or letting them fall into decay. In fact, he needed the wall less for defense than to keep his soldiers from deserting. Thus, the idea of a wall as an obstacle for a city's own inhabitants was not the invention of the German Communists; their kings had thought of it much earlier.

It was Frederick II, known as 'the Great', who undertook the building program that was to make Berlin truly one of the most beautiful cities in the world, and during the 1920s the fourth largest. After 1948 the division into eastern and western sectors led to a duplication of institutions: at the time of the unification of the two Germanys, Berlin had over 100 university and other higher educational institutions, three operas and two theaters for operetta, innumerable libraries, museums and galleries, and two zoological gardens.

As East and West Berlin were a kind of showcase for the two opposing power blocs, the two sectors rose fairly quickly from the ruins and rubble of the Second World War. Whether the haste of rebuilding always produced architecture of lasting value and beauty is another matter, and often a question of taste. In the eastern part of the city, Karl

241. Halle, located in a sandy plain on the Saale River, is an important administrative and industrial center of eastern Germany. Inhabited since prehistoric times because of the valuable saltpans nearby, the site was first recorded as a Frankish fortress in 806. Its renowned university was founded in the 17th century, when the city became a major center of Protestant theological studies. Its most famous son is the composer Handel.

257

Marx Allee was modeled on similar Moscow architecture of the 1930s, when Stalin's dictates and taste prevailed. People made fun of the heavily ornamented, neo-Baroque buildings, but today, several decades later, the street at least looks different from the colorless façades, totally lacking in character, to be found in both parts of the city, in fact everywhere from Shanghai to Vladivostok or San Francisco.

Berlin was the capital of Prussia until 1871 and then of Germany until Hitler's downfall. There are arguments, however, about whether it should be the capital of a reunited Germany. It seems, though, that the decision has already been made, contained in a sense in the agreement that allowed the Democratic Republic to join the Federal Republic on the basis of the West German constitution. This states that Berlin is the capital, but Bonn is the seat of the parliament and government. Will it remain so? Probably until, as agreed, all Soviet troops withdraw from German soil in 1994. Then Germany's most important institutions will be transferred to Berlin. A sure sign is the sudden drop in real estate values in Bonn and their sharp rise in Berlin.

The best known structure, a symbol, as it were, of the whole city, is certainly the imposing classically-inspired Brandenburg Gate, completed in 1791, which served as an entrance to the Berlin of that time. Crowning the gate is a statue of a quadriga, a chariot drawn by four horses abreast. After the division of the city, the Brandenburg Gate was at the western edge of East Berlin, so close to the border it was forbidden to approach it. Now it is a must on every visitor's list of tourist attractions.

Like all of Berlin, the Alexanderplatz, always considered the center of the eastern part of the city, was badly damaged in the war. The East German regime had the surviving buildings torn down and reconstructed the entire square in an undistinguished modern style. Thus, the real center of the reunited city will probably remain the famed Kurfürstendamm, West Berlin's main shopping thoroughfare, with the most expensive shops, most elegant cafés, most exclusive hotels, and nearby the best-known theaters. At its eastern end rises the shell of the Emperor William memorial church, preserved as a reminder of the horrors of war.

Hamburg

Germany's largest city after Berlin, Hamburg (pop. 1,604,000) is a place where three different worlds coexist.

First of all, there is the great port. Though the city is some 90 miles from the open sea, the wide estuary of the Elbe allows oceangoing ships to sail right up to Hamburg. Covering an area of over 620 square miles, the port is 67 times bigger than the principality of Monaco, yet accounts for only one seventh of the city of Hamburg. Passenger ships arrive at the Sankt Pauli docks, and disembarking travelers cross eight large bridges. But the port is so huge and the shipping so busy, it was necessary to dig a traffic tunnel as well. In 1911, 11 million marks were spent on a 1496-foot tunnel under the Elbe. A new tunnel, 11,000 feet long, with six lanes at a depth of 90 feet under the river bed, was completed in 1975.

Sankt Pauli also lends its name to the biggest red-light district in Europe, with the Reeperbahn, a street famed for its brothels and bars. Some of these establishments, for instance in Herbertstrasse, occupy picturesque, old, half-timbered buildings. Another attractive building serves as the local police station, which explains why the crime rate is not higher in this part of Hamburg. The clients are no longer only sailors: visitors, and not just men, come from every continent.

The real Hamburg, however, has little to do with the port, and even less with its night life. The real Hamburg is a patrician city, displaying much more Anglo-Saxon reserve and discretion than any other place in Germany. It was first mentioned as Hammaburg in the ninth century, when it was founded by Emperor Ludwig the Pious. Around 1250, with a population of some 10,000, a fairly large city for the time, it joined the Hanseatic League, becoming after 1510 a 'free imperial city'. It lost its status as a city-republic only occasionally, when occupied by Napoleon, for example, or during Hitler's rule. It entered the German Confederation as a separate entity in 1815, and is today a *Land*, i.e. federal state. Hamburg never recognized an aristocracy – its citizens were even forbidden to accept medals of honor – yet the old bourgeois families formed a distinct patrician class, which on occasion could display more arrogance than any count or earl.

Patrician Hamburg lies on the right bank of the Aussenalster lake (Outer Alster). Here, in fact, a tributary of the Elbe, the Alster, widens into a larger outer and smaller inner lake. The splendid villas here are practically hidden in their private parks. Possibly even more exclusive villas flank the lower reaches of the Elbe in Elbchausee Street. These three cities – the bustling port, the city of entertainment and sexual permissiveness, the city of wealthy burgers – barely notice one another, despite their proximity. But a stranger may have a startling experience while walking along a narrow street past elegant shops windows without realizing that the port is close by. Glancing up, he will suddenly see the funnels and mast of an ocean liner passing before him in what is not a street but a canal.

Hamburg supports one of Europe's oldest and most renowned operas, and thanks to its resident choreographer, American John Neumaier, it also has one of the world's finest ballet companies.

In 1913, poet Paul Claudel, serving as French consul-general in Hamburg, wrote the following: ''Hamburg is a city of truly remarkable character, though there is something shapeless and gloomy about it that reminds me somewhat of Boston. But above it is the northern, maritime sky with green church spires pointing upward like needles of ice.''

Though it suffered heavy damage during the Second World War as a testing ground for fire bombs, the city was soon rebuilt, so that Claudel's description is still valid today.

The port of Rostock, copperplate engraving, late 17th century.

Munich

German poetess Ricarda Huch wrote in 1932: "Neither Munich's location, nor the character of its buildings, can be described as beautiful; nor is it imbued with that ineffable breath of ancient tradition, for its style dates mostly from the reigns of Ludwig I and Maximilian II; nevertheless, it is a city to which the heart cleaves and the eye loves to dwell upon. The University with its fountain, the old Hofbräuhaus beer hall, the green-domed Theaterinkirche, the Frauenkirche in all its grandeur, the Hofgarten park, even the railway station, the Oktoberwiese area, the Nymphenburg palace with its park and the other palaces — who would not feel at home here or, if far away, long to return?"

Much in Munich (München, pop. 1,212,000) has changed since this was written. There is nothing romantic about the railway station, now a meeting place for laborers from distant countries, mostly Turks, Arabs, Serbs, Spaniards, making arrangements, buying the latest newspapers from their homeland — very little German is heard. To the left of the railway station begins the red-light district. Most travelers from afar do not arrive here but at Riem airport outside Munich. The attractive old Hofbräuhaus, too, has suffered a sorry fate, gaining a dubious place in history as the scene of Adolf Hitler's first major political speech.

Even so, Munich as a whole deserves to be called a 'capital with a heart'. It somehow does not seem a part of serious-minded Germany, as if a breath from the Mediterranean had managed to slip past the towering alpine barrier. Here both the locals and their guests take pleasure in the city's famous beer, its 'white' sausages and probably the world's tastiest pork knuckles, while Munich's Montmartre in the charming district of Schwabing has attracted artists for over a hundred years.

It is known that the city was founded by Prince Henry the Lion (Heinrich der Löwe) in 1158. The oldest surviving buildings are the Frauenkirche (Church of Our Lady), finished in 1468, and the old town hall, finished in 1474, both by the same builder, Jörge Ganghofer. The Frauenkirche, with its two tall spires (345 feet) and unusual shallow copper domes, is a city landmark. Visitors who make the climb to the top (permitted only in summer months) are rewarded by a magnificent panorama, on a fine day extending as far as the Alps, 25 miles away.

The great Schloss Nymphenburg, set in its magnificent park, was the summer residence of the Bavarian rulers, the Wittelbachs. It originated in the mid-seventeenth century but was much extended over the next

Disarming the Berlin civic guard on November 11, 1848, contemporary engraving.

hundred years. The lovely circular Amalienburg pleasure pavilion, added in the 1730s, is an outstanding example of the courtly Rococo style. The glittering hall of mirrors in the centre of the Schloss was designed by architect Cuvilliés, who also built the Altes Residenz theater, where performances are still staged in an ornate Rococo setting. The Residenz, a fascinating complex of historical buildings in the heart of Munich, also includes the Neues Residenz theater, home of the celebrated Bavarian State Opera.

Famed for its art as well as its theatrical and musical life, the city has innumerable museums and galleries. The most renowned is the Alte Pinakothek with one of the six largest collections of Old Masters in the world. The Neue Pinakothek exhibits European art, especially German, from the eighteenth century on, and includes a notable collection of French Impressionists. The still prestigious Academy of Fine Arts was founded in the late nineteenth century.

Cologne and Bonn

The landmark of Cologne (Köln) is its cathedral, Germany's largest Gothic church. Though its construction began in 1248 the choir being consecrated in 1322, the vast building, 470 feet long and 245 feet wide at the transepts, was not completed until the late nineteenth century. Its silhouette with two 515-foot spires dominates the entire city. Its interior is adorned with priceless works of art, and many more are housed in its treasury, one of the richest in Europe. The cathedral also has the world's largest hanging bell, St Peter's, weighing 25 tons.

Cologne (pop. 938,000) has been the most important city on the Rhine since Roman times. The ancient Roman military camp founded here around 38 B.C. grew into an extensive town, seat of the Roman governors of Lower Germany. Some of its fortifications and a tower (the Römerturm) have survived, and many more remains can be seen in the extremely well-conceived Römisch-Germanisches Museum near the cathedral. The Roman wall formed the boundary of thirteenth-century Cologne, which had a population of some 40,000, and 150 churches. Many have since been destroyed, but there are still some fine examples in the late Romanesque style.

Just 15 miles up the Rhine lies the small city of Bonn (282,000), served by the same airport as Cologne. It, too, can claim Roman origins, but through the centuries it remained a sleepy, provincial place, home of a prestigious university but otherwise overshadowed by its big neighbor. As the birthplace of Ludwig van Beethoven, whose father traded in wine (always a respectable and remunerative occupation along the Rhine) and the place where another great composer, Robert Schumann, died, the city has significance for lovers of classical music. A picturesque riverside inn, the Schaumburger Hof, has been a meeting place for poets and philosophers since the time of Heinrich Heine.

Thanks to its former mayor, Konrad Adenauer, Bonn became the capital of West Germany, the paramount factor in the city's postwar development. Several former communities, such as Friesdorf, Plittersdorf, Godesburg and Mehlem, have now merged with Bonn, forming a long, narrow conglomeration nestling between the Rhine and the gentle Kottenforst hills. Though the city is maligned as dull and provincial many foreign diplomats posted here find it a very pleasant place to live.

Frankfurt on Main

Frankfurt (Frankfurt am Main, pop. 625,000) is a city of money, art and parkland. Once the capital of German emperors, it is now the seat of the German Stock Exchange. Not far from the ancient city center rise scores of skyscapers – concrete evidence of the city's postwar financial clout. Many older residents regret the change the new skyline has wrought in the character of their historical birthplace, though this is due in part to the bombing and fires of 1944, which destroyed some 2000 medieval buildings. Money has, also regrettably, attracted drugs and prostitution. Gangland fights and slayings, sometimes involving innocent bystanders, are not infrequent after dark in the streets near the railway station.

The chronicles of the city of Frankfurt begin with a historic gathering in 794, when Charlemagne summoned the church dignitaries of the western world to meet with him on the river Main. It is not known exactly when the first international fair was held in the city, but in the Carolingian period it was already a place for the exchange of goods from far and wide. General trade fairs are still held here every spring and fall, as well as numerous specialized events, such as the motor show and book fair.

The city's landmark is its gabled medieval town hall, the Römer (meaning 'Roman'). This originally consisted of 11 separate houses on the Römerburg, which the municipality purchased in 1405 and converted into its *Rathaus*. As the rulers of the Holy Roman Empire were elected in Frankfurt from 1356 on, the town hall has a specially designed *Kaisersaal* used for imperial coronation banquets, hung with portraits of the German emperors.

The fairly modest neo-classical church of St. Paul, completed in 1833, owes its importance to its use as the meeting place in revolutionary 1848–49 of the first German National Assembly, and is considered a symbol of German unity and democracy. Burned down during the war but reconstructed in 1948–49, it is now used only for ceremonial occasions, such as the presentation of the Goethe award (past laureates include Sigmund Freud and Albert Schweitzer), the Peace Prize, and German Book Trade Prize.

Frankfurt's efforts to preserve old values and adapt them to modern needs are illustrated by the Baroque guardhouse *(Hauptwache)*, built in 1729. Blocking traffic, it was dismantled stone by stone and re-erected, several hundred yards from its original site, at the beginning of the Zeil, the city's principal shopping thoroughfare. Beneath the street and adjacent square on four underground levels are subway tracks, and shops occupying 50,000 square feet of space. The guardhouse above now accommodates a pleasant café.

Few visitors who fly into Frankfurt's airport, one of the world's busiest, miss a visit to no. 23/5 Grosser Hirschgraben Street. Patiently waiting their turn at the entrance may be 50 or more camera-toting Japanese tourists, for this is where the poet Goethe was born in 1749. The house is in fact an exact replica of the original, destroyed in the war, but the contents are authentic: the pictures, furniture and paintings had fortunately been previously removed for safe-keeping.

It has been calculated that of all the world's cities, Frankfurt allocates the most for the arts, proportionate to its population. It is justly famed for its museums, many built in the last few decades, all of them boasting generous budgets for new acquisitions, and for its theatrical life.

A popular regional specialty is *Apelwoi* – a wine made from apples – generally available in the old part of the city, Sachsenhausen, with its maze of narrow streets and romantic-looking courtyards.

Leipzig

Only 70 miles from Dresden, Leipzig (pop. 550,000) began as a Slav fishing village in the middle of marshland between the Pleisse and Parthe rivers. Thanks to its location at the junction of important routes, Leipzig flourished as a commercial town as early as the twelfth century, its fairs rivaling those of Frankfurt. Its renowned university, where Goethe studied, was founded in 1409. For these reasons but also because its prospering citizens were not to be outdone by the nobility of nearby Dresden, Leipzig developed in its own way into a city of the muses. Above all, from the seventeenth century on, it was the leading center of book and music publishing in Germany.

The city is perhaps best known, however, as the home of Johann Sebastian Bach (1685–1750), who for over a quarter of a century was cantor of St Thomas's school. It was on the organ of the church of St Thomas that he composed some of the most beautiful music created by man. This church, built in 1212 but much altered in the fifteenth century, contains the composer's tomb. Two of his four musician sons – Johann Christian and Johann Christoph Friedrich – were born in Leipzig, as was Richard Wagner. Felix Mendelssohn, commemorated by a statue in front of the university library, also held a musical post in the city.

In the nineteenth century, Leipzig became an important industrial center, processing steel and manufacturing highly complex machinery. This prompted Ferdinand Lasalle, a friend of Marx and Engels – then living in England – to organize in Leipzig, in 1863, the German Workers' Union, which later evolved into the Social Democratic and Communist movements.

Bautzen, formerly Budissin, in the district of Dresden, 17th-century engraving.

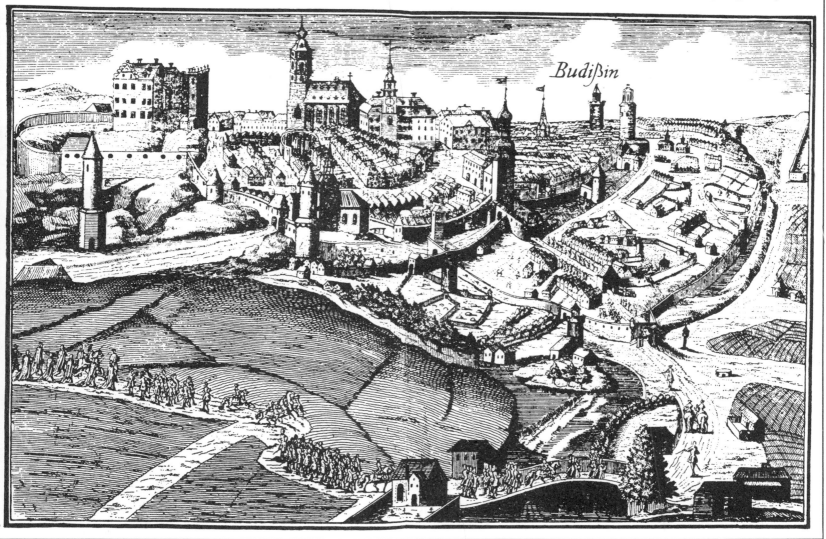

263

Dresden

First mentioned as a chartered town in 1216, from the sixteenth century on Dresden developed as the capital of the rulers of Meissen and Saxony (Sachsen), a royal, then administrative center of southeast Germany. The mines of Saxony gave its rulers great wealth, enabling them to beautify this city on the Elbe and make it a world-renowned center of the arts. Dresden owes much to the colorful, extravagant Elector Frederick Augustus I (1670–1733), known as 'the Strong'. As Augustus II he also became king of Poland, having converted to the Catholic faith to make himself eligible – much to the disapproval of his Protestant Saxon subjects. He demostrated his physical prowess not only in tournaments and many wars but also in his sexual exploits, begetting a host of illegitimate children.

Augustus the Strong was an admirer of the French Sun King, Louis XIV, and his palaces and parks emulated French models. As his main residence he built the so-called Zwinger, an odd name for a palace, for in German it means an enclosed space where animals are kept. The Dresden Zwinger, designed by Matthäus Daniel Pöppelmann, is a rectangular courtyard enlosed on three sides by the wings of the palace. The fourth side was closed in the nineteenth century by the building of an art gallery.

Between February 13 and 15, 1945, Dresden was totally destroyed by bombing (no other German city suffered so much damage), in which an estimated 300,000 people died. Yet within a few decades the city was rebuilt, and in 1964 the Zwinger, restored to its former splendor, was reopened, the U.S.S.R. having returned 750 of the most valuable paintings carried off by the Red Army when it took Dresden. The palace once again contains a priceless art collection, including some of the most celebrated works of great masters: Raphael's 'Madonna of San Sisto', Rembrandt's 'Self-portrait with Saskia', Correggio's 'Adoration of the Shepherds', and many other masterpieces.

A fabulous collection of works of applied art is housed in the Green Vaults (Grünes Gewölbe) Museum. Of special interest are the bejeweled costumes of the Saxon rulers and the gleaming dinner services of gold, silver, and a material that at one time was even more costly. Since Augustus the Strong never had enough money for his expensive tastes, he employed alchemists to discover a way to make gold, setting them up in the nearby town of Meissen, where they were guarded virtually as prisoners. One of these alchemists, Johann Friedrich Böttger, together with the gifted physicist Tschirhaus, experimented with kaolin, found in abundance in the area. Though he failed to produce any gold, he more than satisfied Augustus by discovering a way to make porcelain, at that time obtainable only from China and Japan and worth more than any precious metal. At the Green Vaults Museum his first cups are on display, together with delicate sets of Meissen china, produced without interruption since 1710 at the oldest china factory in Europe.

Dresden (pop. 520,000), straddling the Elbe, 430 feet wide at this point, is one of the most attractive cities in the eastern part of Germany. Its delightful opera house, completed in 1878, presents some of the finest performances of classical opera in all Germany. With a long and illustrious tradition in scientific and technical studies, Dresden is noted for the manufacture of optical instruments and cameras, and also for its nuclear physics institute, directed for decades by the self-taught Manfred von Ardenne, the man who proposed the atom bomb to Hitler, but fortunately was not believed. Von Ardenne later helped the Soviet Union catch up with the United States as a nuclear power.

242. *Statue at the Olympic stadium built for the 1936 Games in Berlin. For the new German leader the Olympics served a political purpose, drawing athletes from all over the world and breaking the isolation closing in on Hitler's Germany. The impressive new stadium was decorated with numerous statues reminiscent of imperial Rome. Interestingly, the style of art and architecture promoted by Nazi Germany differs little from Stalin's 'socialist realism'.*

243. *View of the television tower across the roof of a sculpture-ornamented palace in eastern Berlin. The designers of the tower obviously slipped up in their calculations: as the sun sets in the west, a shining cross appears on the large glass sphere housing the restaurant, an ironic twist for the atheistic former regime.* ▷

244. The Reichstag, parliament building of the German empire, was built between 1884 and 1894 by architect P. Wallota. On February 27, 1933, soon after Hitler's rise to power, the building was gutted by a fire which the Nazis blamed on the Communists, and used as an excuse to suppress all political opposition.

245. Another symbol of Berlin is the Victory column (Siegessäule), which supports a gilt, winged female figure bearing a laurel wreath – Victoria. Raised in 1872–73 to honor Prussian victories between 1864 and 1871, some consider it a monument to German militarism. The column, which stands in front of the Reichstag, is 233 feet high and has steps inside leading up to a viewing platform.

246.   Statue of Richard Wagner in the
Berlin Tiergarten (zoological gardens).
Once a hunting preserve, in the time of
Frederick the Great the area was turned
into a royal park. Today the wooded
expanse with a small lake and streams,
almost two miles long and over half a mile
wide, is a green oasis amid the bustle of
city life. Many other monuments grace the
park.

247.   Façade of the former East German
state opera with the dome of the church of
St Hedwig in the background. The opera
stands on Berlin's most famous boulevard,
Unter den Linden ('under the linden
trees'). Nearby is the theater for comic
opera (operetta). As there are two more
operas in the western part of the city,
Berlin with four opera houses is probably
unique.

251, 252.   For decades, the wall that separated the western part of Berlin from the eastern, was a tangible symbol of a divided Germany. This accounts for the passion that many Berliners displayed, when political circumstances allowed, in trying to tear it down with their own hands. On the western side the Berlin wall was decorated with graffiti. The first holes attracted the curious — peekholes into another world. Today the liberation of East Germany is often called simply 'the fall of the wall'. ▷

253.   Over the years attempts to escape across the Berlin wall took dozens of lives. East German guards had orders to open fire mercilessly. Memorials for sometimes unidentified victims were placed only on the western side. ▷▷

248

248.   In memory of the fearful war fought against Hitler's armies, a monument to Soviet soldiers killed between 1941 and 1945 was raised in East Berlin. Berliners view the monument with mixed feelings. Many think it has no place in the newly reunited city. Others feel that this memorial to the forces that defeated fascism should be preserved.

249.   A guard standing before the eternal flame that burns for the 'unknown soldier' where state visitors to East Germany came to lay their wreaths. The monument is located on the Unter den Linden, the

249

honor guard changed hourly. It is interesting that the uniforms, parade step and military marches of the East German army bore a greater resemblance to those of the old Prussian, and hence Hitler's armed forces, than did West German military trappings.

250.   Typical of Berlin and many other old cities is a juxtaposition of historical monuments and modern architecture. This is especially true of the eastern part of Berlin (in the picture), though similar examples can be found in the western sector.

252
253
254

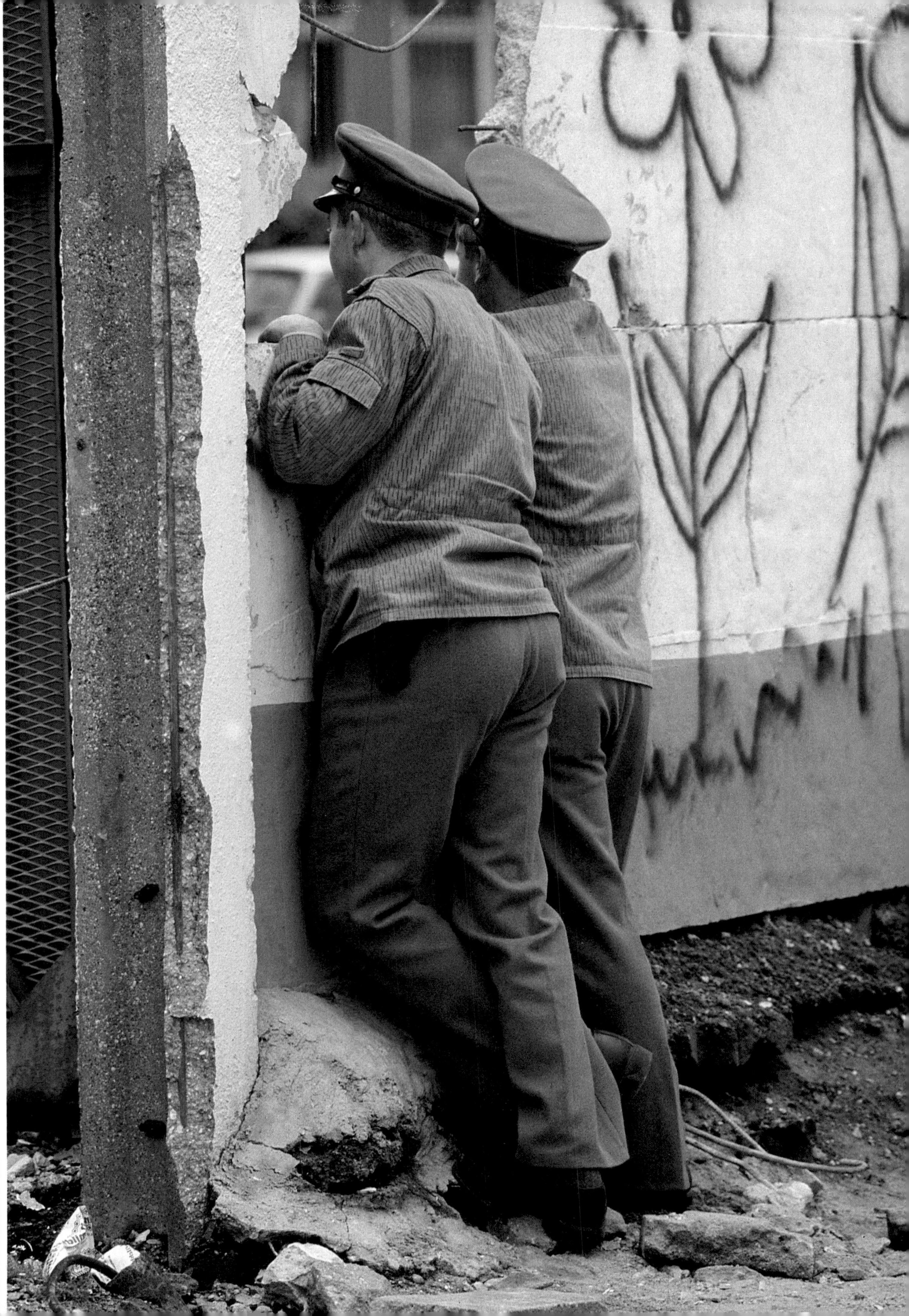

GERMANY REUNITED

THE UNIFICATION OF GERMANY on October 3, 1990, changed the global scene more, perhaps, than any other event since the end of World War II. In a sense it marked the termination of that war, forty-five years after the guns fell silent. Until that moment the political boundary between East and West had cut through the territory inhabited by the Germans, the heart of Europe. This new Germany, born of the union of the Federal and Democratic Republics, now belongs to both the European Community and the NATO pact, to what we call the West. It occupies, however, a special position in view of its separately regulated relations with the Soviet Union, which will continue to station troops on its soil for some time to come, and because of its exceptionally strong economic ties with this country.

As students of German history are well aware, the state created in the autumn of 1990 never previously existed within these frontiers. A good quarter of the former German empire and Hitler's *Reich* now permanently belongs to Poland and the U.S.S.R. In order to achieve unity, Germany solemnly renounced all claims to these territories for all time. This was why a small but vociferous group of German nationalists opposed the signing of a unification treaty with such terms.

In consequence, a certain number of Germans still live in eastern Europe, and some even in the distant Asian part of Russia. Under the West German constitution, which now applies to the whole of the united state, all of them have the right to settle in Germany wherever they wish. As we said at the beginning, Germany has never been a country with clearly defined ethnic or political boundaries, nor the state of all German-speaking peoples. Austria, it is true, was one of the German states until 1866, a member of the German confederation like Bavaria or Prussia, and for long the Austrian Habsburgs provided emperors for Germany. Switzerland, on the contrary, would have nothing to do with Germany, or Austria, after its heroic struggles for independence in the fourteenth century, although the majority of Swiss are German-speakers (69 percent).

Life in the united Germany follows the pattern established in the Federal Republic – not surprisingly, since it was the desire of the East Germans for a western system of government and life style that brought about the downfall of the East German regime. Moreover, West Germany was much larger and more populous: around 70 percent of Germany's present territory of some 137,000 square miles, and over 60 million of its 76 million inhabitants were governed by Bonn.

The new state has retained the federal system of West Germany, not the centralized East German model. The Federal Republic had 11 states or

254. Berlin, October 3, 1990: celebrating unification before the Brandenburg Gate. Events had moved forward at a dizzying pace. In October 1989 the first demonstrations in Leipzig spread throughout the German Democratic Republic. On October 18, Erich Honecker, state and party leader, was forced to resign. On November 9, the East German government announced free travel – inhabitants of East and West Berlin could henceforth cross the frontier freely, which hundreds of thousands did the very first night. ◁

255. Fireworks illuminating the Brandenburg Gate on October 3, 1990. A reunited country was certainly the desire of virtually every German. The emergence, however, of a larger and economically more powerful Germany in the heart of Europe raises numerous questions which only the future can answer.

Länder: North Rhine-Westphalia, Bavaria, Baden-Württemburg, Lower Saxony, Hesse, Rhineland-Palatinate, Schleswig-Holstein, Saarland, Hamburg, Bremen, and West Berlin as a separate district. To fit in with this administrative structure, on the eve of unification East Germany was divided into five *Länder:* Mecklenburg-West Pomerania, Thuringia, Brandenburg, Saxony-Anhalt and Saxony. Some of these federal units had a long tradition of statehood, but the majority were demarcated in a fairly arbitrary, administrative fashion. Significant is the absence from the new map of the name of Prussia, the state that played a dominant role in German affairs for some two hundred years, its kings from 1871 bearing the title of German Emperor. This could be explained by the fact that most of the former territory of Germany which is now part of Poland and the Soviet Union may also be considered Prussia, historically speaking, but the main reason for avoiding this name is probably its association with German militarism and past wars.

Though life in East and West Germany differed in many ways, long before unification the values and aspirations of their peoples, the dreams they dreamed, were very similar. Much of the credit – or blame – for this must go to West German television, which could be viewed in virtually the whole of the Democratic Republic. Thus, East as well as West Germans, and indeed the majority of Europeans, were exposed to the influence of American soap operas. How far their picture of capitalist affluence, the life style of Denver or Dallas, affected the attitudes of Germans living east of the Elbe would make an interesting study for social psychologists. With equal interest the East Germans watched the western commercials, coveting the consumer goods advertised.

The German in the east lived in a paternalistic state where 'someone else' took care of where he would live, what schools his children would attend, what medical care he would receive. With a much lower living standard, but assured of at least the basic necessities, he usually put less effort into his work than his neighbor in the west. In the merged economy of the united state, differences between the former East and West Germans have become even more noticeable. Before, the German in the east was the poor relation living abroad; now he is the equally poor, but much more envious, relative living under the same roof. This situation is likely to continue for some time, until the living standard evens out.

In East Germany there were secure jobs for all, though full employment was maintained artificially: industry was overmanned and a huge number of people were unproductively employed in the bloated state administration. Moreover, working parents were relieved of worries about child care. The East German state made far better provision for this, in the way of crêches, kindergarden and extended stay at school, than the Federal Republic. Its citizens, though denied many of the freedoms of west Europeans, enjoyed a degree of social security and certain rights they had to forfeit as the price of unity. What may be hardest for them is the thing they wanted most: to make all their own decisions. They can no longer put all the blame on the authorities, enjoy a childlike freedom from responsibility, and do only what they are told.

In fact, workers from the eastern part who take jobs in western firms are often dissatisfied, and so are their employers. In the German market economy, a beery night out with the boys is no excuse for getting to work late, nor will employers tolerate just taking a day off or feigning sickness because of urgent private business. Managers from West Germany now running some former state enterprises in the east are often in despair for the same reasons.

Albrecht Dürer: woodcut, 1510, showing a stern Scholar teaching pupils, already with the aid of books.

Another source of dissatisfaction is the difference in the earnings of people with the same qualifications doing similar jobs. The expert in the west often gets double the salary of his counterpart in the east. Added to this, competition on the labor market is now much more severe, so that the undisciplined or simply less skillful worker can easily find himself out of a job. To the former citizens of the Democratic Republic, this has come as a shock. This was not how they imagined freedom. There can be no doubt, however, that they will gradually adjust, and adopt the same attitude to work as the Germans of the west.

But the western Germans themselves admit they are not the workers they used to be. The German artisan, once famous as a master of his trade, can now, in many cases, only replace broken parts, seemingly unable or unwilling to understand the totality of the object he is working on. In factories as well, he keeps strictly to his specific task, and expects to be well paid for it. His union sees to that in the annual round of negotiations with employers. Thanks to the ever healthier state of the economy, the bargaining is mostly over how to split the profits between the owners of capital and the workers, now usually called 'employees'. Though the former take a larger share, percentagewise, the workforce is satisfied to be getting a steady increase in its purchasing power. Generally speaking, there is no close tie between the employee and his firm. His main concern is not the welfare of the company but the improvement of his personal living standard. In this he differs from his Japanese counterpart, a fact that may help to explain why many Japanese goods are superior, and sell better even in Germany itself.

Craftsman casting type, woodcut, 1568.

Rising earnings in any case mean greater spending power, and increased profits for manufacturers of consumer goods. The critics of the 'consumer society' are not few in number, but nothing can deflect the German from his determination to acquire more beautiful furniture, a better video-recorder or camera, a larger house or apartment, and, above all, the latest model of automobile. This last is not just a means of transport but an indicator of his success in life and his view of the world. In every civilized country there are speed limits even on modern highways, but in Germany these cannot be enforced. Any government that tried to do so would be doomed. No amount of official warnings about ecological damage or the volume of traffic accidents can stop the German motorist from zooming along the *autobahn* at 100 m.p.h. or more if he has a car capable of such speeds. In this respect the former East Germans differ not at all. Abandoning their Wartburgs and Trabants, they made it their first priority to buy a western car, sometimes even before securing a regular income.

Only a nice house with a garden ranks higher than the automobile in conveying social status. The West German will spend much of the leisure time for which his union fought beautifying his car, his home and, especially, his garden. A whole industry supplies him with electric mowers and sprinklers for his immaculate lawn, barbecues, garden furniture and pools with a Hollywood image. Likewise, the East German, despite a certain official disapproval, was more often a house-owner than the citizens of other East European countries, and with the same devotion cherished his automobile and his, generally more modest, home and garden.

In recent years Germans have become more open and sociable, and less thrifty, though they still like to put off major purchases until the big summer and winter sales, when last season's model may be a half-price bargain. Many habits have changed as a result of increased foreign travel and the influx of foreign workers *(Gastarbeiter)* from Italy, Spain, Yugoslavia, Turkey and elsewhere. These foreigners, and their children in the schools, talk more loudly, laugh more, dress more colorfully – all of which has had some impact on the 'hosts'.

Not only have they developed a taste for the more exotic food served in Chinese, Japanese, Greek and countless other foreign restaurants, but the standard of home cooking has much improved. Younger people, in particular, take a lively interest in the culinary art, as witnessed by the many flourishing magazines on gastronomy and the huge output of cookery books. In the lean postwar years the main thing was to fill the stomach with meat and vegetables, specially potatoes, all covered in thick, tasteless sauces. Now, in the battle to keep slim and healthy, the modern German has abandoned this stodgy diet and aims to consume as few calories as possible, but in the form of food of the highest quality.

Drinking habits have likewise changed. Throughout most of Germany, except for some areas in the southwest, near the French and Swiss borders, the main alcoholic beverage is beer, and beer-drinking almost a cult. But wine consumption has been steadily rising. Previously the preference was for sweet wines, perhaps because the grapes grown on the steep slopes along the Rhine and Mosel have little natural sugar, and it is in man's nature to desire what is not readily available. Formerly a lot of sugar was added to these wines, a practice that is now strictly controlled, as in France. In any case, wine used to be drunk more often between meals than as an accompaniment to food, and a glass of semi-sweet or even sweet wine was more satisfying when meeting friends just for a drink. Tokay was thus the type held in highest esteem, while French Chablis and red Burgundy were little known. The upper classes, of course, have always been as much connoisseurs of wine as those in other countries.

Certainly the gourmet's reservations about German cooking are now outdated, for good food can be found even in small places and city suburbs, not only in expensive downtown restaurants and five-star hotels. Germans like to eat out, and do so a lot. The tax-deductable 'business lunch', mostly a male preserve, is such a widespread institution that restaurants have a ready supply of the special receipts needed for claiming expenses. To show off his wife's culinary skill – or his house and garden – the German is more likely than, say, the Frenchman or Briton to invite a casual acquaintance home for a meal.

Nowhere is there greater dedication to domestic pets, especially dogs, which are allowed on all forms of transport and in all shops except food stores. There are no strict regulations about fouling public footpaths – at least as far as dogs are concerned. Generally speaking, though, cities are impeccably clean, and the standard of public utilities is uniformly high. Public transport, even at peak hours, is less crowded than probably anywhere else in the world. Many municipalities are experimenting with free transport on streetcars and the subway, to reduce the use of private automobiles, the main cause of city traffic congestion.

In recent years there has been a marked improvement in the formerly abrupt, not to say hostile, attitude of public servants. In their contact with the public, the police, customs and tax officials, post-office and bank clerks, public transport employees and the like, are correct and polite, except when dealing with persons they consider insufficiently civilized. Representatives of the law and public services will be most polite, it is true, toward persons dressed according to conventional bourgeois standards and – even more important – who speak in an educated manner. 'Learned people' are much esteemed: public opinion surveys have shown that Germans have the greatest respect for university professors and bishops, while politicians, successful business people, artists and sportsmen rank much lower down the scale. Those whose speech betrays their foreign origin – the *Gastarbeiter* – fare the worst. The German even tends to be suspicious of a compatriot from another part of the country, a fact usually detectable from his accent.

The well-educated German is recognisable by his syntax, his choice of words, a certain style of diction, though he will still usually retain at least a trace of some local accent. A German Professor Higgins, like the philologist in George Bernard Shaw's *Pygmalion*, would have little difficulty in telling where a person was from. Most modern German dialects differ in accent and the pronunciation of a few sounds, but some are almost unintelligible to the majority of German-speakers. In the north, mostly close to the Baltic and North Sea, the *Platt* dialect is spoken. Close to the Scandinavian languages, it is quite unlike modern standard German, though most *Platt*-speakers know this as well. In the southwest, where people mainly speak *Schwäbisch*, also hard to understand, the problem of communication is greater since the less educated sections of the population cannot express themselves in standard German at all. There are other, less baffling, differences: Berliners pronounce G as Y, for example; Saxons, who speak *Sächsisch*, have a highly distinctive accent and pronounce P as B.

The year 1968 was a major caesura in the life of postwar Germany. The waves of unrest that swept through Europe were particularly turbulent in West German universities, and had some repercussions in East Germany as well. Chairman Mao was in fashion, and Che Guevara's portrait hung in every student's room. The slogans were: "Don't trust anyone over thirty!" and "Beneath the *talar* [academic gown], a thousand years of mold!" The healthy, good-looking, well-fed youth of West Germany, able to travel around the world and read whatever they liked, wanted to break with the bourgeois life style of their parents, but also to draw a line between themselves and previous generations bearing the stigma of two world wars. This gave the events of 1968 a rather different slant from that in other western countries. But here, as elsewhere, they also represented a revolt against the rat race, an outdated bourgeois moral code, and narrowness of all kinds.

It is hard to say why the atmosphere of the 60s evaporated so quickly. The appearance of AIDS in the early 80s had its impact: life was

The town of Wollgast, not far from the present German-Polish border, copperplate engraving, late 17th century.

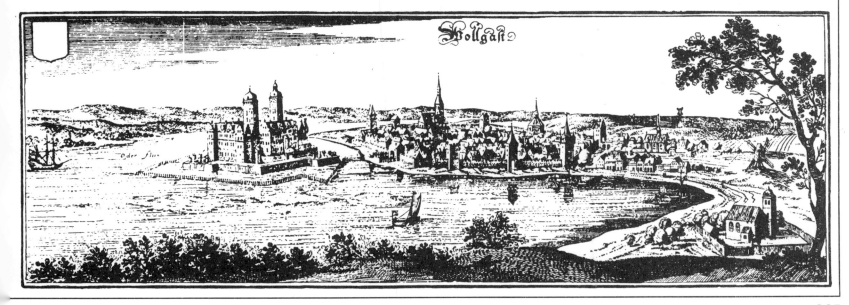

too good to gamble with. Many prominent members of this generation are now university professors, mayors, leading politicians, prosperous businessmen. From the good old days they have kept rather longer hair, often beards, and a more relaxed style of dress: under their academic gowns, worn on official occasions, there are often jeans and tennis-shoes bearing fashionable labels. They look back on their rebellious youth with a bitter-sweet, ironic nostalgia. Their student children, products of an 'anti-authoritarian' education, have nothing revolutionary in their make-up. On the contrary, they aspire to become Yuppies, more interested in improving their own status than society and the world at large.

A few of the most militant members of the 60s generation, impervious to the lure of material comforts, formed the Red Army Faction – otherwise known as the Baader-Meinhof Gang. Their fight against capitalism took the form of kidnaping and slaying prominent businessmen and politicians. At the beginning they were not without their sympathizers, but the ruthless and senseless brutality of their methods better served the interests of the political right, which called for 'law and order'. The original and best-known members of this group have long since disappeared from the German scene, but from time to time their followers still re-emerge to carry out spectacular, and technically highly sophisticated, assassination attempts, some of them successful.

The unification of the two German states took almost everyone by surprise. In retrospect, it seems to people in Germany and abroad that the apple dropped from the tree when it was ripe. In his book *Angst von Deutschland* (Fear of Germany), published in late 1990, the West German writer Patrick Süskind described his feelings about the event:

''Fear? No, that's not the right word. If someone experiences a great shock, it cannot be said that he is overcome by fear. But he feels a certain uneasiness, like a man traveling in a very fast train on an uneven track through territory unknown to him. I have only some vague anxieties. Not the old one, that Germany might sink again into barbarity and *folie de grandeur*, as in the 30s and 40s. But I worry about the possible appearance of major social tensions, much envy and smaller-scale conflicts within the country, and that not only here but further east, where the Soviet empire is crumbling, this might lead to new wars and civil strife.

''Yes, and when I think about it, I am also a little sad that this boring, unloved, practical, little state, this Federal Republic of Germany, will no longer exist.''

This was the farewell of a man who never previously expressed any love for his state, who was immune to any feelings of nationalism, and who once wrote, ''It was all the same to us whether Germans would live in two, three, four or a dozen different states.''

Even President Gustav Heinemann, when head of the West German state, revealed a similar attitude in his famous reply to a journalist's question: ''Do I love Germany? No, I love my wife!'' It is this changed national mood, epitomized by Willy Brandt's spontaneous genuflection before the war memorial in the Warsaw ghetto, that has helped to make Germany deserving of unification and full membership of the great family of free, democratic nations.

Long ago, Konrad Adenaur, first chancellor of West Germany, remarked, ''Our state is not complete.'' Now Germany is 'complete' as a state, united at a time when it is relinquishing some of its national sovereignty and specific features in the name of a much broader, supranational community. This surely marks not just a new chapter in German history, but a whole new book.

'Dropping the Pilot', cartoon by Sir John Teniel from 'Punch', March 1890.

Important Dates in German History

9	Battle of the Teutoburger Wald, in which the Germanic Cherusci tribe led by Arminius (Hermann) wipes out three Roman legions.
98	Tacitus publishes his *Germania,* the first historical work describing the Germanic tribes.
768	Charlemagne (Karl der Grosse) becomes king of the Franks.
800	Charlemagne crowned emperor by Pope Leo III.
1077	In the struggle between emperor and Church, Henry IV is obliged to go to Canossa and submit to Pope Gregory VII.
1190	Emperor Frederick I Barbarossa dies in Asia Minor on the Third Crusade.
1226	Teutonic Order of Knights establishes itself in Prussia.
1273	Election of Rudolf I, the first Habsburg emperor.
1348	First German university founded by Charles IV, in Prague.
1356	Charles IV promulgates the Golden Bull, whereby seven electors will in future choose the emperor.
1456	Gutenberg Bible printed.
1517	Martin Luther posts his 95 theses on the door of the castle church in Wittenberg.
1521	Luther, outlawed and his writings banned by the Edict of Worms, takes refuge in the Wartburg castle, where he translates the New Testament.
1555	Peace of Augsburg sanctions the co-existence of Roman Catholicism and Protestantism in the German empire. The following year Charles V abdicates.
1618–48	Thirty Years' War, a religious conflict that turns into a European struggle for power.
1701	Electoral prince of Brandenburg proclaims his realm the kingdom of Prussia.
1756–63	Seven Years' War: Prussia under Frederick the Great emerges as a major European power.
1815	The *Deutscher Bund,* a confederation of 39 German states, established at the Congress of Vienna.
1848	First elected German parliament meets in Frankfurt.
1862	Bismarck appointed prime minister of Prussia.
1870–71	Franco-Prussian War; Prussia's victory enables its king, William I, to be proclaimed German emperor at Versailles.
1890	Bismarck, imperial chancellor, forced to resign.
1914–18	First World War. After Germany's defeat, William II flees to the Netherlands and abdicates.
1919	Weimar republic established.
1933	Hitler becomes chancellor and *Führer* of Germany.
1939–45	Second World War. Germany occupied by the four great Allied powers.
1949	Federal Republic of Germany established on the territory occupied by the three western powers, and German Democratic Republic in the Soviet occupation zone.
1990	Reunification of Germany.

Index

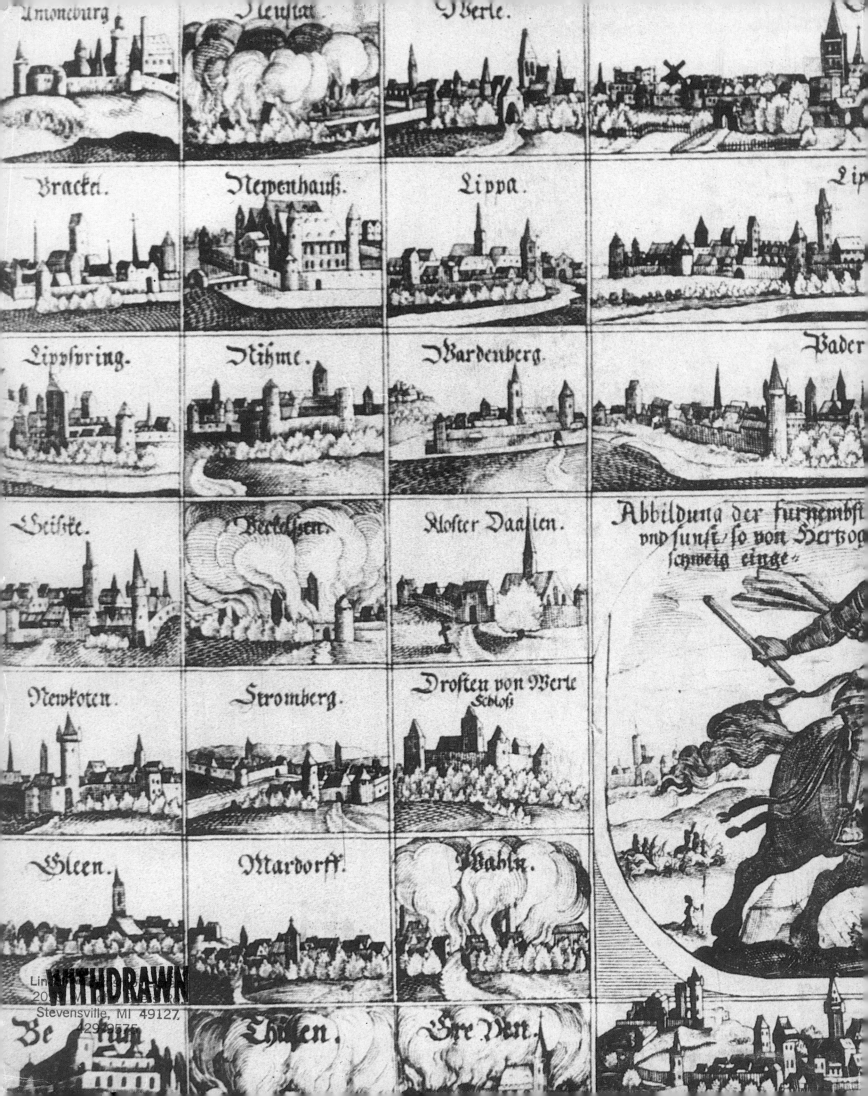

Antoneburg. Newstat. Werle.

Brackel. Newenhauß. Lippa. Lip

Lippspring. Nihme. Wardenberg. Pader

Weiste. Bertelsen. Kloster Daalien. Abbildung der furnembst vnd sunst so von Hertog schweig eing

Newkoten. Stromberg. Drosten von Werte Schloß

Gleen. Mardorff. Wahln.

Be Thälen. Bremen.